AN EARTH-CAREFUL Way of Life

Christian Stewardship and the Environmental Crisis

LIONEL BASNEY

INTERVARSITY PRESS
DOWNERS GROVE, ILLINOIS 60515

InterVarsity Press® is the book-publishing division of InterVarsity Christian Fellowship®, a student movement active on campus at hundreds of universities, colleges and schools of nursing in the United States of America, and a member movement of the International Fellowship of Evangelical Students. For information about local and regional activities, write Public Relations Dept., InterVarsity Christian Fellowship, 6400 Schroeder Rd., P.O. Box 7895, Madison, WI 53707-7895.

Cover photograph: Richard Brown/Tony Stone Images

ISBN 0-8308-1322-5

Printed in the United States of America

Library of Congress Cataloging-in-Publication Data
Basney, Lionel.
  An earth-careful way of life: Christian stewardship and the environmental crisis/Lionel Basney.
    p. cm.
  Includes bibliographical references.
  ISBN 0-8308-1322-5 (alk. paper)
  1. Human ecology—Religious aspects—Christianity.
  2. Environmental degradation—Religious aspects—Christianity.
  3. Conservation of natural resources. 4. Environmental protection.
  5. Stewardship, Christian. I. Title.
GF80.B39   1994
261.8'362—dc20
                                                  94-410
                                                    CIP

15	14	13	12	11	10	9	8	7	6	5	4	3	2	1
04	03	02	01	00	99	98	97	96	95	94				

For Ruth,
Claire and Lauren

Acknowledgments

So personal a book, so long in the brooding and hatching, must owe debts to all sorts of occasions where specific thanks would make no sense. But I have a few debts that need to be named. My wife and daughters are the immediate community of the book. They are the center of which my writing and thinking are the periphery. They are in the garden.

My mother loves flowers and taught me to love them; my father loves wilderness and taught me to love it. I was an "environmentalist" long before the word showed up.

I owe a long debt of friendship to Jack and Linda Leax, our oldest coconspirators in a couple of rackets, writing and gardening. I need to thank Rodney Clapp of IVP, who said, "Yes, I know, but send it along anyhow"; and the editors who published some of this prose first as essays.

Lowell, Michigan
Winter 1993

Introduction

SMALL TURNINGS

This is a book about the environmental crisis. It argues that to understand the crisis, we must reflect on our material way of life, the one we assume; and that to deal with the crisis, we must change the way we live.

No environmental crisis would ever have occurred, however, without a cultural and spiritual crisis: to talk about the first is to talk about the second, and vice versa. The most significant, least avoidable evidence of our cultural and spiritual failure is that our children cannot safely eat the food we give them, or safely breathe the air.

The crisis of planetary life is not simple, or easy to face. Its daily events seem frightening but often far away. The steady advance of African desert, the dumps of radioactive slag, the disappearance of wild salmon from the rivers of the Olympic Peninsula—we know about these things, but we resent being made to feel guilty about them. And of course we are right, in a sense. There is a limit to responsibility. No one is guilty of everything.

Or we may feel stunned by the size of the danger. Some writers believe that we are facing (in Bill McKibben's phrase) the "end of nature" itself. "Are you as afraid as I am?" says the circular in the morning mail. We may feel like answering, "Yes, of course; but what's the point? Things like the end of nature are too big for me to handle." We are right again. The name of fear without hope is paralysis.

Our fear makes us hope for simple solutions—quick, clean, technical solutions. But the problems are not technical any more than they are cultural and spiritual—so to hope for a simple solution is a mistake.

We do of course have some technical solutions for specific needs, and could put them into practice. Many are intellectually complex and inventive. That is, an earth-careful way of life does not mean some kind of voluntary barbarism. We can have science, elegance, sports, children, hot baths, the worship of God and a sane ecology.

What we cannot have, any longer, is the way of life we have chosen and idolized. If we are determined to live frantically mobile, energy-expensive lives, lives carried on in the frenzy of consuming, then no inventiveness will save us. This is because there will shortly be nothing left to save. A culture of consuming can function only as long as there is something to consume. But on a finite world such a culture will eventually come in sight of the end of consumables. That is where we stand now.

The only thing to do now is to learn, and begin, to live in a different way.

The Rake and the Worldview

By "we" I mean those of us who live in the postindustrial Northwest of the world and participate most fully in its culture. If I were writing to an Andean potato farmer or to an Amish farmer, I would say something like "Don't change, or change very carefully; and teach us."

Some cultures have made preserving the earth a primary duty. I don't mean to idealize them. They are no more perfect cultures than any other. But it is desperately ironic that we, whose way of life makes consuming the earth primary, should have thought for so long that we were better off than the others, and should teach them. It is our way of life, not theirs, that has done the harm.

As I write this, it is fall. The brilliant leaves are coating the lawns. A couple of hours ago someone said to me, "It's a beautiful day," and I responded that I needed to go home and rake leaves.

"We probably should too," he said. "But we're not going to," and I was struck by the pleasure, the exultation, in his voice. I don't know what he was going to do instead, and the remark was not serious. But in a sense that was its importance.

Probably he thinks of raking as an aesthetic thing. It makes his lawn green, like the others. In another way of life, the fall and its changes would be practical concerns. Fall would be time to do necessary work, work that obligated us and defined our responsibilities. But behind his words was the confidence that that sort of work was not necessary, not his concern; and, implicitly, that nature was not his concern. The technological culture had freed him from all that.

If I had asked for his environmental opinions, they would, I'm sure, have been impeccable—all about resources and waste and the glory of God in creation. But none of this had come home to him; or he had taken none of it home *with* him.

I did not tell him about leaf-raking in my own small vegetable-garden economy—how the composted leaves lead to the fresh produce we are still eating, every day, in October.

Nor did I tell him about my pleasures—the sweetness of the air, the clarity of the wind, the daughters who still come to help for the pleasure of talking as we work; the courage of my elderly neighbor who, eighty and unwell, facing death, has bought a new wheelbarrow and rake and is out at work; the tiny myrtle flowers I uncover; or the hand-smoothed handle of the spraddled rake as old as my daughters and still in use.

It is true, in a sense, that we are facing a crisis of worldviews, that Descartes and Newton and Nietzsche stand behind it. But there are more immediate causes. What has led us here is the decision, made long ago but confirmed every day in our practice, to transfer responsibility for nature onto machines, and to build ourselves a cocoon of manufactured goods from which to defy necessity.

It can be done, by a few people, for a little while. But not by everyone, and not for long. It costs too much; nature suffers too much, and as nature is not the background of our lives, but food, heat, air and water, the sufferings of nature will inevitably be shared by people. At the moment they are being paid for largely by Third World people, who labor and starve for our extravagance. But nothing in the records of civilization suggests that Americans cannot starve, or that the poisons we have mainlined into the world will not poison us as well.

Power

A great deal is being written about the environmental crisis. Some of this is theological—work to recover the scriptural basis for an earth-careful way of life. Some of it is topical—one hundred things you can do to save the earth.

Much as I value both kinds of work, this book does not fall in with either. I have not written theology, or a study of the Bible, or a defense of a specific social minority or a call to a particular social cause. All these are implicated in my thinking. But I have tried here to do something more concrete—to think about how our normal ways of providing for our normal, unavoidable needs have brought us this way to disaster.

I chose to write about this because I thought that reflecting on how we live may help us to change. But what is the energy of the change, and what is the form it will take?

"I can do all things through Christ who strengthens me," a student quoted to me one day in some irritation. If I recall correctly, what she wanted to do was become head of a corporation. Her point was that *doing things* was itself a neutral activity, which she could fuel with the power of Christ.

She was thinking like a good child of the technological culture. One of its central ideas is that energy is an abstract and perfectly adaptable thing—that the energy we use puts no conditions on our use of it. So we strip-mine for low-grade coal to burn for electricity, and burn our lights late into the night, without wondering where the coal comes from, or what strip-mining does, or what people pay for our convenience.

But power defines your use of it. You can't run a bulldozer on solar cells, or at least not yet. You can't plant seeds with a nuclear explosion. You can't starve someone else's children, or burn a rainforest, or head up a corporation that does, through the strength of Christ. It cannot be done that way. If *that* is what you want to do, you must train yourself to ignore the Source.

We might say, then, that our task is to discover what we *can* do "through the strength of Christ"—with that power, but also under that constraint. This is going to mean, ultimately, changing the basic practical principles of our way of life.

We may insist that our task is to "redeem" or "transform" culture. But it is pertinent to ask what we intend to transform it *into*. You can't transform a culture just by joining it and doing as it does in Christ's name. There are things, many things, that postindustrial Western consumers do that cannot be done under that Name.

Many of these, further, are things that we have been used to doing, and have thought were permitted, normal. It's our normal way of life that needs examining. The examination will need to be fresh, practical and particular: of course we need to change our opinions—but also how we eat, travel and use time.

We are faced with the burden of "living in the strength of Christ" *and not otherwise;* and this qualification may put what seem to be stringent limitations on what we can do. But if the environmental crisis means anything, it means that we will not live much longer unless we live in the right way, with the right constraints, in the right freedom. It is blessedness or death. No substitutes need apply. The substitutes for blessedness have cost us almost everything.

Turnings

As I said, this is not a theological work. It is not a book *about* belief; it has been written *within* belief.

Two verses have been constantly in my mind as I wrote. One is Revelation 4:11, in which the elders say to the Father that the cosmos exists "for thy pleasure" (KJV) or "by thy will" (NEB). (Brahms set the verse to the great fugue in part 6 of his German Requiem; most of the time I remember it in that form.) The Scriptures' unquestioned rule is that nature and humanity exist by the word and for the purposes of God. This disposes of the idea that nature is ours to do with as we please.

The other verse has no musical setting that I know of. It is Galatians 6:2—"Carry each other's burdens, [because] in this way you will fulfill the law of Christ" (NIV). This is the basic rule of practical ecology, human or natural or human-in-natural. And we cannot carry each other's human burdens in any responsible way unless we carry nature's as well—as nature, after all, carries us.

This book was not written in a library or a study. (The pages in chapter three attacking consumerism were written, I confess, in the business library of the University of Kentucky; this was just mischief.) It has been written in my car, in airports, on the dining room table; a good deal of it was written in the garden, whose virtues it extols.

I have read a fair amount of specialist work, but have no ambition to contribute to it. I have not read as a specialist in "environmental concerns," but as a human being in danger. This is how we ought always to read when the work is important. You read theology (for instance) as a human self in extremity; this is how you read great poetry and philosophy. Their concerns are too urgent for any other treatment.

I don't have much of comfort to say. I think our task at the moment is to face the pain of our situation and not turn away from it. You cannot repent in ignorance. First the law, that makes things clear; then repentance; then the new life.

Any change deep enough to protect life on the planet will have to be a repentance. It will have to be that concrete. No "deepening" consciousness, no change in "perspective," no keeping back with the Joneses will do. We will have to turn directly around in the places where we stand.

Realistic confession, honest repentance, concrete restitutions. Small, specific, practical turnings.

P.S.: On Terms

I've found it difficult to know what to call the main object of my reflection in the following pages. I've settled on *culture*—more concrete than *worldview*, far more concrete than *perspective*, broader than *lifestyle*. To this noun I have attached a series of modifiers representing our culture viewed in different ways.

The "technological culture" is more than machines or what Jacques Ellul calls "technique"; it is our culture in terms of its faith that advancing technology can be trusted to take care of our practical needs. The "consumer culture" is the same culture seen in terms of our consumption of nature and the products of technology; the "cheap-energy culture," our culture in terms of its dependence on the consumption of fossil fuels. These are not separable things. They are one way of life. Without mass access to fossil fuels our technology would be unimaginable and our consumer goods impossible. Start with any of the three and you reach all of them, in short order, in the same way.

1
In the
AISLES
of
PLENTY

"IF THIS SHOULD STAY TO DINE," HE SAID,
"THERE WON'T BE MUCH FOR US."

LEWIS CARROLL

H*ere is a story about the environmental crisis.*

A Soviet woman was visiting an American city. It's safe to guess, I think, that her feelings were mixed. She wished to be courteous to the American couple who were being courteous to her; but she was full of the defensive patriotism Soviet people often felt, and of the Soviet public sobriety, so she did not seem much impressed with what she saw. She withstood the eight-lane highway with its endless, sleepwalking lines of cars. She was courteous about the shopping mall.

Finally, the tour over, she and her guides stopped at a supermarket. There, unexpectedly, her composure faltered. Standing in the narrow aisles of cans and cereal boxes and liter bottles and jars of sauce, before the heaps of waxed apples, she just stared for a moment. Then, overcome, she began to weep.

In the Soviet Winter

The story has two morals. The first is the one you have already thought of, the one attached to the story when I first read it in a magazine. According to this moral, the story is about one moment in the conflict of systems that has obsessed us for so long, and still does: capitalism against socialism, free enterprise against state control, individualism against communalism, civic freedom against the suppression of opinion. That is, the story is about the superiority of America.

But how is it a story about the environmental crisis?

It is, because it is a story about food. The picture of the woman weeping in the supermarket is only partly, or shallowly, a political picture. She was not, at that moment, a Soviet citizen. She was a human being who had known need, facing an overwhelming abundance. She was a member of a more limited society than ours, an unaffluent society, one with few surpluses. Therefore she saw, more clearly than did her American friends, hurrying after their pound of hamburger and gallon of milk, what meat and drink mean.

Even the political meaning of the story depends on something older and deeper than political thinking: the struggle of humans everywhere, always, just to live. This is the larger story that gives the political one its significance. Political questions come home to us because they concern how we will live—whether we will be safe, whether we and our children will have enough to eat. And all such questions are environmental ones.

Now, of course, all of the political issues have changed. Someone has shuffled the deck. As I write, the Soviet Union has become the former Soviet Union. That vast political ambition has torn itself apart; its enormous economic power is bogged down in the contradictions of theory and bureaucratic administration. American theory, American politics, seems to have won the day.

It would be a mistake, however, to see all of this simply as the defeat of one ideology and the triumph of another. Politics is environmental: it is concerned finally with subsistence. The two contrasting ideologies have always been tied together by one industrial use of nature: they have agreed that nature means resources to be exploited.

When the Soviets began buying American grain in the mid-1960s, the two systems began to lean on each other in a way that made the political uses of the earth obvious. The Soviet government bought grain to feed its citizens—and thus to justify itself in their minds. The American government sold grain to keep our economy expanding—to justify itself, therefore, in our minds.

The Soviet Union has fallen apart now, in great measure, because it could not solve the problem of subsistence. Our supermarkets seem to prove that we have solved it. But we have in fact maintained our affluence by overstressing our environment, by overproducing, by wasting soil and water. It is ironic, then, that the Eastern European nations, newly autonomous, are flocking to join Western financial institutions such as the World Bank. Financially it is inevitable: and yet these agencies have on their books desertified African grazing land, destroyed watersheds and the burning of the Amazon forest.

Part of international politics today is participation, willing or not, in this damage to the earth. What political question can we ask that does not have the earth as a principal component? A domestic question such as the state of the economy echoes in every wetland with potential for real estate development, in every small coal-town; a foreign policy question, such as limited war to contain aggression, bristles with the probability that environmental damage will be used as a weapon or suffered as a consequence.

Though politics and economics have always been ecological matters, however, something has changed. It has always been true that farmers who increase production lower consumer prices, and politicians get elected in the glow of good times. In the past almost no one thought back down this chain of consequences to the cost, in the field, of increased production. The change is, now, that this cost has become too great to ignore. We must think back to the field.

Not that we don't ignore the cost. We do; and this gives most of our political talk, in this time of astonishing changes, a dazed quality, as if we were sleepwalking, like the cars on the freeway. We keep telling ourselves we are going toward freedom and prosperity. That's not what the road signs say.

Oats at Waterloo

But why start with a story about food and not something else, such as oil?

There are several reasons. The first is that the connections food makes between the earth and culture are permanent and necessary. When the oil runs out, or when it becomes too scarce and expensive to use, we will do without it, as we did for centuries before its commercial discovery. When food runs out, nothing can replace it; everyone who wants to go on living must eat.

This gives food a kind of natural priority in any sane environmental discussion. When we start with something else, such as oil, we are starting at a second step. Oil is one of the resources necessary for industrial food production. But we could do without it if we were willing and able to grow our food in a different way. To start the discussion with oil, then, is to begin by assuming our present ecology, wasteful and destructive as it is.

Food moves us beyond this assumption. It sets the priorities straight. When the British journalist William Cobbett insisted that the calamities of the farm laborer in 1820 took precedence over those of the Manchester factory worker, he was not arguing out of nostalgia for the countryside. His point was logical: without bread Manchester would cease to exist, indeed in a matter of weeks. The same was true of Rome, which from 123 B.C.E. guaranteed every citizen (not women or slaves) a daily allotment of grain. (Hence the bread in "bread and circuses.") The same is true of New York, Moscow and Beijing.

It is useful to think about food, then, because everything else in culture depends on a reliable and permanent supply of human and animal nourishment. Culture is, initially, a way of making sure of food.

Moreover, food is in some ways a surprisingly stable thing. When you eat a dish of oatmeal, you are eating one of the oldest classes of food—raw or roasted grain pounded, or rolled, and mixed with water: what the Greeks called *maza*, the Romans *puls* (hence, in the English of Shakespeare's day, "pulse") and the Tibetans *tsampa*. It was eaten in Neolithic times, and in Sumer; by the European poor, as a staple, through the eighteenth century; as "stirabout" by Wellington's army the rainy morning of Waterloo.

Something that does not change is a clear sign of changes around it. This genealogy of breakfast cereal shows us one thing historians are always remarking—that we are culturally further from Waterloo than it was from Sumer. Our oats have been prepared by machine, not by hand or animal or tool. The machines are driven not by food energy but by coal, oil and electricity. At Waterloo agriculture was still delivering a calorie of food for less than a calorie of energy; now our calorie of food costs us ten of energy. We are not eating the earth's good surplus; we are eating the earth itself.

Finally, food organizes culture (to use Ruth Cowan's distinction) both horizontally and vertically. Growing, collecting, transporting, processing and selling food gather many technical systems, many places and people, on a single horizon. But a given food can be a focus for a whole way of life: rice in the East; potatoes in the Andes; coffee in corporate and academic America. Tea in Great Britain is a drink, a daily meal (that is, a biological and psychological rhythm), a family touchstone, a social lubricant, a cause of war, trade and colonial politics. Would you do business with someone who wouldn't drink tea with you?

All this seems prosaic and ordinary. This is exactly why I have brought it up. However great the dangers we face, we have raised them around ourselves by doing prosaic, ordinary things. These are what we must understand and may change. We need to find a better way of thinking about ordinary things such as how we obtain food. We need to think, that is, about supermarkets.

The Food Museum
The store is a bright, lively place, clean, well-lighted, designed for broken-field perception—signs, banners, red tags shouting "SALE," cans in walls and pyramids, smiling, handsome faces on eight-foot posters. The sections of the store are color-coded, each aisle marshaled according to food type and kind of display: shelves, the bins and tables of fruit, the high frosty cabinets of desserts, the vegetable freezers. Things are easy to find, easy to buy.

Necessaries—milk, butter, eggs—are in the rear. This draws you through the store, past other things that might attract you. As you go you see that it isn't exclusively a food store. A lot of what is here isn't food—shoe polish, aspirin, mousetraps, greeting cards, videos. The cashier's chute is surrounded by gum, candy, cough drops, television guides and the magazines that sell the pornography of curiosity.

It is undeniably impressive. Sprinklers come on, periodically, to produce little false rains over the peppers. Small track lights glow over the piles of green apples as if they were shrines. It's only when you look up beyond the track lighting that you remember you are standing in a big iron shed with a cement floor.

The supermarket got started when A&P chain stores began to replace local shops during the Civil War. So long ago, we began to give away responsibility for subsistence to organizations larger than we could control or influence. The first true supermarket opened in 1913. The plan was financial, for lower overhead—let the shopper do for herself, or more rarely himself, what clerks had been paid to do before.

But, ultimately, there was more to it than that. The supermarket organized the distribution of food nationally, and then internationally. It drew on the technology of canning and freezing—Gail Borden first condensed milk in 1856, Clarence Birdseye sold his quick-freezing method to General Foods in 1932—on mass transportation of foodstuffs and on the irrigated year-round growing of fruit and vegetables on Bureau of Reclamation land in California and Washington. Food could be guaranteed (within reason); handled in mass quantities, indefinitely storable, it could be organized like the supply of automobile parts, like any other industrial product.

It is odd that the supermarket mostly ignores two of our senses. Except for cubes of cheese on toothpicks, no one expects to taste anything at the food store. Nor, except occasionally in bakeries and fish sections, do you smell the food. Too much is in cans. The fresh vegetables are too cold, the meat is plastic-wrapped.

For that matter you don't touch much of the food or weigh it in your hand. Most of the fruit and vegetables are packaged, so that when you reach for pears you touch a metal can covered with paper. The label wears the picture of a pear. But it isn't the pear you are buying, or even (now that you look at it) much like any actual pear. It is too perfect, too consistent, the color is too uniform, too like ink. It *is* ink.

Much of the food is hidden. The carrots seem to be in a transparent bag, but the windows have been tattooed with orange stripes—the expected color, of course, but hard to see past. In a curious way you seem to be buying not food but packages. You don't judge the goodness of food but the information printed on the labels—not something concrete, that is, but something abstract, words, statistics.

It doesn't change matters that the statistics represent ingredients and nutritional information. The stricter the government is about labeling, the clearer the basic message: you cannot trust what is in the can. You haven't seen it, smelled it or tasted it. You know nothing about how it was grown. You must accept the numbers; you have no other choice.

Shopping here, therefore, is an act of faith, where faith should not be required. What becomes of faith when it is demanded, enforced? It becomes suspicion. We cannot help being suspicious. Too many machines, procedures and opportunities for making money stand between us and the field. We have lost the chance, and the ability, to judge for ourselves.

Excess

What does the store teach us about food? First, and most obviously, that there is plenty of it—that the shelves will always be full. This is, in one sense, a blessing beyond reckoning—it was what made the Soviet visitor weep—but it has a profound unconscious effect on us. This flood of food, these aisles full of enough and too much, are as much a cultural symbol as the fact that "good" restaurants always serve you more than you can eat. Both examples of excess keep us from remembering that food is grown in limited quantities—so many acres, so many ears of corn.

The drive to surround ourselves with excess comes in part from the fear of scarcity—a universal fear that has shaped more history than have kings or wars. This fear last shaped American policy in the fifties and sixties, when the Depression generation determined that its children should never know need. It has been our boast for decades that Americans enjoy plenty, that our food supply is the envy of the world. And the icon of that envy is the supermarket.

The consciousness of need, however, is one of the beginnings of wisdom. For need is a constant in human experience—you meet it every morning before breakfast—but plenty is the human exception. Our having so much too much effectively separates us from most of humanity in other times and places. Our norm is the abnormal.

It teaches us to believe a falsehood: by freeing us from scarcity, our food supply has eased out of our minds the principle of limitation. We forget that both we and nature are limited—we, in what we can safely do, and nature, in what it can afford us. We believe that the possibilities of human action are infinite.

But it is not only the absence of need that teaches us this false freedom. We began to disbelieve in limitation almost from our first landfall on Cape Cod. What the American frontier meant, in ecological terms, was apparently inexhaustible quantities of trees, animals, fish, ore and room. Audubon watched, stunned, as pigeons streamed in a dark flood above his head for days. Our imaginative response was to leap from quantity to infinity, and to think that nothing we could ever do would lessen the possibilities.

Of course this is not true. We might say conservationists are people who have grasped this fact, which the rest of us have not. It would help us to face an empty shelf in the supermarket. An empty shelf is a sobering fact; and there are many peoples in the world more sober than Americans.

A Hundred Feet of Pop

A second significant, deceptive fact about supermarket food is that you can have it any time you want it. This also is profoundly unnatural. Nature goes by season, and native peoples, such as Gary Nabhan's Papago Indians, had metabolisms adjusted to seasonal diets. Our technologies of farming, supply and storage give us year-round consistency of diet: the head of lettuce in January. Your parent or grandparent (if she lived in the north) thought an orange at Christmas a treat, a kind of miracle. Now it is part of our (unnatural) national norm.

Third, the food in the supermarket is not in anything remotely like its natural condition. Seventy-five percent of it will be processed before it reaches the store; processing uses more than twice the energy every year that agriculture uses. The food will have been treated to artificial purification and convenience portioning and packaging; it will have been sorted, filleted, cleaned, softened, pasteurized, homogenized, precooked. It will have been made user-friendly. For some of it the only proper word is *manufactured:* think of the more bizarre cereals (Corn Crickets and Choco-Anarchy) and "processed cheese food substitute."

Food, that is, has become something whose goodness is guaranteed not by nature but by industrial process. Unless it is in California, where the section will be larger, the store will have a small corner for organically grown vegetables, relatively expensive. Mostly, however, we desire the machine's intervention. We are afraid of nature. The bag of lentils has a label that says, "These are products of the earth; clean them before you cook them." I do, in fact, sort through the lentils. But it is not the occasional corn kernel or flower seed I am looking for; it is the shred of metal from the processor.

The mark of food's industrial status is its uniformity. If the peas or fruit pieces are of different sizes or "irregularly shaped," the package will say so: otherwise we might think the system had failed. Yet the irregularity of peas, or apples, is one of the most natural things about them.

The peas are a long way from the pod, however, conceptually as well as in miles. The industrial food-system functions to keep the life of the field and the feeding-pen (which provides the life in the food) as far from the kitchen as possible. The evidence that food is, as Bruce Colman says, "seeds (grains), leaves, fruits, meats, and roots" has been carefully removed.

Fourth, the food in the supermarket seems to be enormously varied. This is not false to the facts of food itself—humans have eaten thousands of things—but to the facts of our food. For the apparent variety in the supermarket hides a drastic simplification.

The seventy-five feet of breakfast cereal come down to four grains—oats, rice, wheat and corn. These resolve themselves further into the predominance of corn, which is the basis of many "multigrain" cereals and the sweetener of many. The one hundred feet of soft drinks and snack foods are full of corn sweetener and corn meal shaped into horns and curls. Most of the corn grown in the United States, finally, feeds the animals whose flesh fills the meat freezers.

This simplification hides another, more dangerous, one. A quarter of American cropland grows corn. And a year's corn will be genetically reducible to a few strains—which makes the crop as a whole drastically vulnerable to drought, disease and pest. We are, theoretically, only a few degrees or an insect species away from empty shelves.

The apparent variety in our food, then, is overwhelmingly industrial. It is something we manufacture from the "ore" of corn and rice. To become an "ore," food must be ruthlessly simplified; natural variety must be ignored or even destroyed; the breeding and nurture of many species must be replaced by the mass production of one or two.

Examples of this manufactured wealth and natural impoverishment abound throughout the store. Perhaps the most familiar example is the apples. In their bins and heaps, fruit-waxed glossy, the apples are all of three or four species. Yet in 1850—before the first A&P store—there were a thousand American varieties, a thousand flavors, shapes and colors. Many had been bred for marketing before it became clear that the modern market preferred mass production of a few varieties. They exemplified a culture that was profoundly horticultural, that longed to live within a fruitful nature. There were apples so distinct and vivid that they had the names of other fruits: Early Strawberry, Lyman's Pumpkin Sweet, Sops of Wine.

The largest category of apple Thoreau knew, however, was winter apples—the ones that wintered well, that cost no energy to store. Each apple—Flowering Chinese, Limber Twig, Dominie and Seek No Further—came from a single region, as a given wine can come from one field or a given cheese from one valley. These varieties are all but forgotten—quite forgotten by the supermarket, which does not need to husband energy. It is an irony of our food that what we take to be a wealth of possibilities is in fact a humbling poverty.

Clockwork Oranges

The supermarket is a transparent display of the workings of technological culture. It is a place where we impose our conscious pattern on nature and on ourselves. Reaching across the continent for food, processing it, boxing and canning and wrapping it in plastic, passing it through the system of distribution, putting a price on it, designing its displays, advertising it, we are having our will with things. We are making food what we want it to be.

The most striking fact about the system is how far it puts us from anything we could justly call "natural"—the field, garden, orchard and barn, and the plants and animals that grow there. The distance is first physical—the typical molecule of American food travels thirteen hundred miles to get to the lunch table—but then, inevitably, conceptual. Both the consumers of food and its organizers (who are also consumers) are absent from the natural place. The natural fact is simply not present to us; we are not aware of it; it is not alive in our minds.

Moreover, this absence, first physical and then conceptual, has practical results: when we come to think about nature and how we are to treat it, we discover that we know it only abstractly—at a distance. It is not surprising that our thinking about nature is naive and riddled with errors.

Behind the supermarket—the motor, so to speak, behind the dashboard—is modern agriculture. This is sometimes called "industrial agriculture," meaning that it uses industrial products, machines and chemicals. But this is the right name for other reasons. We believe that agriculture is a branch of industry; that it is a technological problem.

In ecological terms, industry means extraction. Without ore and oil we would have nothing to make machines out of or run them on, and nothing for machines to manufacture. Thus, the modern economy is extractive: the old Soviet Union paid for food with oil and gold, as do the OPEC nations. The Philippines prepared for the horrifying floods of 1991 by extracting forests from their watersheds.

Modern agriculture works on the same model. It too is, at base, extractive. Soil fertility is treated as ore: the violence of farm machines extracts it from the passive field. Once extracted, the food-product itself is a raw material, a neutral "stuff" like crude oil, to be transformed into a marketable commodity. The corn that costs so many bushels of Iowa and Washington topsoil to grow is itself only the medium for what manufacturing does to it to "turn it into food." What is left after the process is, naturally, "waste."

The industrial model for farming lies behind other assumptions that we have made about food. The first assumption is that world hunger is best confronted with measures to increase bulk production; and therefore that the solution to world hunger is best worked out in those parts of the world, such as the American Midwest, where production in quantity is easiest to achieve, no matter how far this is from the store.

The second assumption is that food production, in bulk, ought to govern our choice of means—large technological solutions, such as fertilizer and pesticides in bulk, swarms of machines and rivers of oil to drive them.

Another assumption is that food, like other things, is best handled not by people but by machines, that people are always replaceable by machines, and people's wisdom, memory, affection and intuition by data and spreadsheets.

Fourth, the authority for deciding on food ought to be in the hands of agencies suited to organizing large solutions and the money it takes to run them—namely, international agencies and governments.

Finally, the person who works on the land—the one potentially in touch with nature and natural fertility—will be best provided for by being brought into the mass economy like any other consumer; and best utilized by becoming a replaceable part in the production machine.

These have been our assumptions for five decades at least. But they are not necessary assumptions; they are not the only agricultural ideas available. Gary Snyder appealed to a different set altogether when he spoke of the "detailed understandings" of soil and water needed for "the delicate propagation of plants which are sensitive to the finest variations in climate and soil." Industrial agriculture assumes that all farmland is essentially the same, and therefore that the same procedures (with variations in hybrids and herbicides) will work everywhere. That is, the land is regarded as the same kind of "stuff" as raw food.

What Snyder implies is far closer to the facts of the planet—that arable land is enormously varied, and that to fit crop to land and climate wisely and tolerantly depends on "detailed understandings." This would mean working with nature, not against it; it would be nurture, not extraction; it would challenge every farmer's intelligence, in the details of its place. It would be organized locally, not globally; it would put responsibility for the earth back into the hands of the people closest to it.

The Company Farmer

But we have been traveling the other way for a long time—for longer than the five decades that industrial and chemical farming have been the norm. Farmers have long been expected to contribute to much that was not in their interest, to carry the burden of social demands that they had little share in formulating.

From the first, farming in the new world was designed for its usefulness to the old. Every major intermission in Europe's ability to feed itself—industrialization itself, or the recurrent wars—produced a boom on the American farm market; every peace treaty signed in Paris produced a slump in Chicago. American farming, that is, has from the start been understood in terms of what it would contribute to an economy located off the farm and out of the countryside. Farmers have been primarily required, as Donald Worster says, not to look after the land but to increase the common stock of money.

But the profits from farming have seldom enriched the farmers themselves. In 1837, it took 148 man-hours to raise an acre of wheat; in 1890, it took 37. The profits from this fall in overhead costs, however, went for industrial expansion. The most important decisions about farming, therefore, were made in markets, government offices and corporate boardrooms.

These agencies have always idealized the American farm family as the source of American prosperity and independence. At the same time they took out of the farmer's hands the power to say what would be grown, how much and when. The farmer became a dependent of the system. The idealization of the farm family and their work was the same as other imperialist idealizations, the British image of the happy Irishman and the Russian autocratic image of the holy serf. What the Irish shepherd, the serf and the farmer knew—the "varieties of climate and soil," the local conditions and long traditions of work—was sacrificed, like the people's humanity, to the cause of industrial expansion.

The ecology of farming has been sacrificed in the same cause. The assumption has been that economics and technology will set the agenda for nature: that the economy will spend, and nature will pay. Neither industry nor the market can, of course, produce a single carrot or a slice of beef. If we want food, we must turn to the natural endowment of fertility and animal growth—what E. F. Schumacher called the "irreplaceable capital which man has not made, but simply found, and without which he can do nothing."

But industrial agriculture hides the nature of nature from us. Its implicit principle is that we can go on endlessly spending the fertility of the soil just as we can go on endlessly accumulating interest or multiplying the stock of dollars.

Interest, however, consists of numbers; farmland and its fertility exist in actual fields. Numbers can be multiplied indefinitely; there are only so many arable acres in the world, and fewer each year. It is obvious, then, that fertility will be spent long before we finish accumulating numbers. To judge agriculture, or any other use of nature, exclusively in terms of what it contributes to the stock of monetary wealth is to subordinate it to an impossible standard. It is judging apples as if they were zeros. It replaces natural conditions with cultural expectations. The result can be, has been, catastrophic.

The most recent agricultural "breakthrough," the biotechnological revolution, makes this clear. New genetic strains tailored for specific places and climates would seem to be working with nature. In fact, these strains are utterly dependent on industrial products—new varieties to replace constantly degenerating ones, new chemicals to feed and protect the plants and to replace vanished natural immunities.

The unnaturalness of this is not hard to state: too much of the natural process has been replaced. The proof is that the system will not sustain itself. It is in constant danger of deterioration, and is constantly degrading its own environment. It needs constant mechanical and chemical attention. These crops, someone said, are like terminal patients on life-support systems.

Left to itself, a healthy native polyculture will draw and hold its own water and nutrients, control weeds and insect pests, provide for its own propagation and build up the fertility of its soil. These powers are the signs of natural health.

That is, the polyculture will do for itself what it would take a well and a mechanical pump, a herbicide and pesticide program, artificial pollination and chemical fertilizer—all produced, distributed and run on fossil energy—to do for it. These dependencies are the signs of unnatural manipulation; they are the signs of working against nature.

There is a common conviction, then, behind agricultural decline and the rest of the environmental crisis. It is neither a scientific result nor a philosophical conclusion. It is a belief lived out in the supermarket aisle: the belief that we can reduce the supply of human needs to a problem soluble, without remainder, by enough ingenuity and enough power. But the belief is a fallacy.

Figuring the Costs

Has industrial agriculture been a success? Our answer depends on how we figure; and, as many voices have pointed out, two methods of figuring exist.

One is essentially financial. Addressing itself to international GNPs, it tells us that the world's economic productivity has quintupled since 1950. Addressing itself to agriculture, its all but exclusive concern is production. By this kind of accounting, industrial farming has been an unparalleled success. The world grain harvest in 1984 was 2.6 times greater than in 1950. Grain production in the United States went from 130 million metric tons in 1950 to 330 million in 1982—or from 1.6 metric tons per hectare (about 2½ acres) to 4.2.

Even here, however, some doubt arises. Since 1984, grain production has shown no annual increase; in 1988 it began to shrink. Between 1970 and 1985, staple food production fell behind population growth in fifty-three developing countries. African grain production has fallen 20 percent from its peak in 1967. This shrinkage, combined with population growth, has meant that almost three times as many people were undernourished in 1985 as in 1975.

The distance between the GNP figures and those for food constitutes what Lester Brown calls the "illusion of progress." What is revealing is that this distance is the same, fundamentally, as the distance between the supermarket, which represents the fruits of industrial agriculture, and the human and natural costs of producing food. In both cases the cultural evidence is, so to speak, opaque. We see it, and do not see the natural harm behind it.

What we think of as prosperity—that is, increase in industrial capacity and consumer spending—has come, since World War II, at the expense of our capacity to feed ourselves. Agricultural land and water have been diverted in vast quantities from agricultural use. Rural people have been driven into the urban work force. Where these changes are going on most quickly, as now in Asia, the disappearance of self-sufficiency in food is most dramatic. Our envious idolatry of the Japanese, for instance, might be qualified if we noted that from a peak in the seventies, Japan's grain production has shrunk by 25 percent.

The folly of economic progress at the expense of food—the folly of swapping bread and rice for VCRs—is obvious enough in itself. We would see it clearly if the ingenuity and pleasure of the VCR did not get in the way. We know, abstractly, that food does not come from technology and economics; yet we focus on them as if it did. We amass the power to imagine, control and profit from food, at the expense of food itself. We are preparing to sit, hungry, in front of a video image of bread.

Clearly we need another kind of accounting, one that accounts for the natural and human resources of our lives. This accounting would ask what our gigantic gains in agricultural production have cost: cost both the earth and the farmer.

The numbers here are grim. We are losing 24 billion tons of topsoil a year, worldwide, to water and wind erosion. In the former Soviet Union somewhere between 500,000 and 1.5 million hectares of farmland a year are being abandoned to wind erosion alone.

Any adequate accounting of this kind would add farmland poisoned by overused fertilizers, pesticides and herbicides; farmland sterilized by salt from irrigation; water poisoned by run-off from poisoned fields; irrigation water and aquifer reserves wasted by irresponsible pumping.

The human costs are likewise great. During the seventies government policy in the United States encouraged farmers to contract debt for land, machinery and chemicals. Farm debt more than doubled between 1972 and 1982; by the early eighties, interest payments on farm debt bled off nearly half of all farm income. At the same time, land values fell by as much as 39 percent in six Midwestern states. By 1986 farmers were failing at the rate of fifty thousand a year.

The name of these numbers is the "demise of the family farm." Along with the idealization of the American farm family has always come a sentimentalization of its troubles. But the implications are in fact practical, because of a principle we will come back to again and again: the health of land in use depends on the immediate attention and care of the users. The small farm worked by a family is not just a political and social ideal. It, or something like it, is a practical necessity, because it provides a stable link between the state of the earth and human care.

Wendell Berry has been the most insistent observer of this principle. He has repeatedly reminded us that the preservation of the knowledge of farming depends on the maintenance of farm families and farm communities; and the land's continuing fertility depends on this as well.

This connection makes the decrease of America's rural population—from 30 million people to 5.4 million between 1900 and 1982—an ecological disaster in itself. What Wes Jackson calls the "eyes-to-acres ratio" has changed to the point where arable land is not being maintained because it is not being *seen*.

None of these shortcomings of American agriculture is American alone. For one thing, the industrial world has been practicing American agriculture for some decades. Rural economists and sociologists are now talking of an international farm crisis arising out of the demands made on farming by growth economics and industrial technology. The collapse of land values that bankrupted American farmers in the 1980s drained Australia's best farmland of 40 percent of its value in two years.

Ecologically, world agriculture is stretched now to the breaking point. Gene Logsdon has remarked that American farmers fail when a stretch of bad weather removes their immediate cash flow; they have no margin, no elasticity. The same is true of world grain production. What began its downturn in the mid-eighties was not mismanagement but drought.

The successes of industrial agriculture have been like the successes of industrial systems in other things; and the costs have been the same. This agriculture has enormously increased production of a few commodities; it has increased economic activity on the national scale and the temporary comfort of many people. It has cost the long-term devastation of farmland and the impoverishment and cultural degradation of many other people. It has cost us something else, less concrete but perhaps more important: the widespread knowledge of nature and how to live within it. A human generation, on several continents, has grown up unable to see the fields on which their lives depend. The supermarket is standing in the way.

Syrup with No Syrup in It
I went into a primary classroom in mid-March and found that the teacher had designed a unit on maple syrup: books and enlarged photos, a small

table set with pancake mix, a waffle iron and a bottle of syrup. But the photos, with their horse teams, piles of split wood and sap buckets, misrepresented sap gathering as it is done today—most sap runs into plastic sacks, or down plastic tubing to galvanized tubs—and there was, in fact, not a drop of maple sugar in the syrup. It was mostly corn sweetener.

I am far from suspecting the teacher of bad faith. It was plain that the lesson had practical and pious intent: here is nature; here are the people who do the work; here is the result—taste it. It may even be that the teacher knew the lesson was inaccurate: that the photos were used out of nostalgia, and the syrup bought on the run. But the display incarnated our national ignorance about nature. Even when we want to come back to it, we don't know where to go.

We think we do: we go to "tourist farms" set up, as a recent Chicago editorial said, "as a reminder of a precious heritage sacrificed to inevitable growth." A heritage that has been sacrificed, however, is no heritage at all: it no longer exists. To have a heritage you must carry it on; you must do, in some sense, what was done before. Not every culture has a heritage. Every culture has a past. But to a culture committed, as we are, to "inevitable growth," the past is just dead. It is something you keep in a museum.

I read recently, in a petroleum company's quarterly magazine, about a "nature preserve created"—one presumes with company money—"minutes from busy downtown Calgary." But what does "preserve" mean in this context? Has it been preserved from the pollution of the city only minutes away? Is it large enough (how could it be, just minutes from the city?) for species to establish their own ranges and biomes? Nature has not been preserved, in any generous or ecologically self-sufficient way. It has been put in a museum.

The tourist farm will tell you as much about farming as industrial syrup will about maple trees, a supermarket about food and a nature preserve about wilderness. In all these cases we have cut nature down to museum size, and have, consequently, only a distant and superficial acquaintance with it. When we ask questions about nature, then, we give the wrong answers, not because our intentions are bad, but because we can bring no sense of nature to bear. We have no sense of nature. We have been deprived of our senses, in relation to nature; and therefore of common sense.

This is why we think of the environmental crisis as something destroying the flora and fauna of distant continents, or think we can deal with it by setting up preserves and making nature films. Of course we ought to do such things. But preserves and films are examples of museum vision. They distract us from the marrow of the problem, which is how we do what we must do to live.

How we do what we must do—how, for instance, we feed ourselves: we do not feed ourselves, really, or pay any knowledgeable attention to the sources of food or how they are being used on our behalf. We are inclined to believe that all such problems have been solved, and that things we used to depend on—modesty of ambition, reverence for the earth, the patient "seeing to it" that enriches fields as they feed us—are unnecessary now, now that we have machines to look after us.

The result is that the fields are being destroyed, and the irreplaceable vitality of forest, grassland and arable land—on which all human life, in all its cultural variety, depends—is being lost. The result of that, inevitable though we postpone it, is cultural collapse.

For there is a sense in which the Soviet woman with whom we began had been conned by the supermarket. She wept because she thought the store meant infinite plenty, endless resourcefulness. We think so too. We are both wrong. The supermarket is not a success, but a failure. It means plenty only temporarily, and at great cost. Ultimately, it means famine.

2
The
MARRIAGE
of NATURE
and
CULTURE

YOU MAY BEGIN BY SAWING THE LITTLE
STICKS, OR YOU MAY SAW THE GREAT
STICKS FIRST, BUT SOONER OR LATER YOU
MUST SAW THEM BOTH.

HENRY DAVID THOREAU

*T*hinking *about the environmental crisis in terms of an everyday*
humdrummery like a supermarket has one great advantage. It makes us
face the fact that the crisis, like human life itself, is a matter of nature and
culture, or of culture-within-nature. Any explanation that tries to divorce
the two misses the point.

We can, of course, pry nature and culture apart for the purposes of
definition. Complicated as they are, we might begin: nature is what the
universe has in it before culture arrives—nature is soil, wind, DNA, the
constant speed of light, the processes of decomposition—and culture is
what humans do, or make, with nature in building a human world—cul-

ture is row planting and combines, a taste for orange juice or snails, ten-day diets, violins and capitalism. Every effort to define nature is, of course, a cultural action. Still we know the umbrella from the rain, and probate law from the law of gravity.

Since diets assume food, however, and violins are made of wood, the distinction needs some reinforcement. We might describe nature by saying that it has only one loyalty, to its own created ways. This is what is implied by the Chinese word for nature—*zi-ran,* self-thus. A Christian would change this slightly: self-thus because made-thus. The point in both cases is that nature has, so to speak, a single mind; left to itself, it knows what to do. A forest ecology finds an evolving balance of species and nutrients, and then looks after itself. More than the "laws of nature," which are cultural formulas for nature's dependability, it is this "looking after itself" that is nature's mark. To be what it is, to be the delight of the One who made it, it does not need our interventions or (for that matter) us.

Culture, by contrast, has two loyalties. It has a divided mind. Like nature it has its own laws and histories. New thought answers old thought; Aquinas talked back to Aristotle, Walt Disney to the Brothers Grimm. Inventions set off other more complicated inventions.

But culture is also loyal to nature. It cannot exist outside nature or provide for its own needs. Culture will be more faithful to nature, in the long run, than to itself, because if it leaves natural conditions too far behind, it will collapse: it will starve itself, or poison itself.

To say that culture cannot do without nature, further, is to say that *we* cannot do without it. Modern civilization has built such elaborate webs of culture around us, we have intervened in nature so drastically, that we sometimes think that culture *is* humanity. But nature is as close to us as the blood in our veins. What we know as human life is made up of nature and culture in dense, complicated cooperations. We live at their intersections.

A field of wheat is natural and cultural at the same moment and on the same acre. There is the soil, which we have not made and only in part understand. There is the digging stick, hoe, tractor or genetic variation, whose conception and form are human.

We not only do live at these intersections; we must. Too far out either limb, nature or culture, and we die. We cannot live on Beethoven and no rice; on the other hand, we cannot live in a blizzard without a coat, a hut and an artificial source of (natural) fire. The tolerances of human survival are fairly narrow.

Though we typically think of the environmental crisis, then, as a natural event—animal species decimated, forests burned, air gummed up—any strand of the crisis that we pick up will lead us into an unbroken fabric of natural and cultural events. The death of wild salmon runs in Washington rivers has been accompanied by industrial events, such as the exploiting of hydropower and nuclear energy; by ethnological events, such as the destruction of Native American cultures; by agricultural events, like the creation of irrigated farming on a large scale; by financial events, such as the shift of capital to the Northwest and the resulting depression of other parts of the country; by the growth of supermarket chains.

The death of the salmon has been justified, further, by beliefs in the power of human intelligence to solve all problems; by moral judgments about the superiority of money to tradition; and finally by religious convictions about the status of human beings in the creation and the expendability of other beings.

All the connections in this dense list could be traced out in historical detail. They make up the story of the fate of those marvelous creatures, the king salmon and the coho, once the technological culture started to work on them. But the lesson for today is not that we can remove this history and put everything back the way it was. Too many effects are now in place. The lesson is that we must think carefully, urgently, about what to do now.

Culture Alone

If our crisis is a matter of culture-in-nature, then clearly there are two ways of turning our backs on it. One might be called "culture alone." The other is the advocacy of "nature alone."

The overwhelming inclination of technological culture is to declare its unilateral independence of nature. We want to think, we do think, that human designs and inventiveness can ordain the conditions of human life—that we can make the world into anything we like, and that to deny this is to deny human freedom.

"Human freedom" is both political and spiritual, of course, and I mean both. Our cultural investment in technology is so profound that it blurs such distinctions. That our economies depend on growth and growth on new gadgets is almost too obvious to mention. Our politicians, however, mention it all of the time. This is because our hope for a governable world rests on technology too: if all economies grow, and if all humans are tied into a global communications web, then the causes for war will evaporate. That is our political faith, and—since today we invest most of the emotion we used to invest in God in the dream of a secular peace—a religious faith as well.

It will turn out, eventually, that consumer economies cannot grow forever, and that technology cannot replace all natural conditions with its own. For the moment, however, we cannot believe this, partly because technology is so omnipresent and so near. All of us put our trust in it in irrational ways.

We live, for example, with a constant proliferation of machines seen as good in itself. New dorms at major universities have to accommodate increasing flocks of small machines following the students to school—sixteen electrical outlets per room, at UCLA, to fuel (as *The New York Times* listed them) "two computers, two compact disk players, a 19-inch color television, a microwave oven, an answering machine, an electric shaver, a popcorn popper, a coffee machine, two electric alarm clocks and a refrigerator." That is in each room.

Part of a UCLA education, then, is the implied lesson that the world can afford no end of machines. But we Westerners are, or should be, the people most aware of the vanishing resource base of civilization. We know that the fuel is limited; that the only reasonable tactic is lessening, not increasing, our demands. The electrified dorm room, therefore, small as it is, has the quality of a dream, or perhaps of psychosis, a taking leave of reality.

Similarly we are geared up, now, to graduate engineers and scientists at a faster rate—not in order to find effective solutions to specific environmental problems, but in order to guarantee a growth economy, which must feed, of course, on the same shrinking stock of fuel as the dormitory ravenous for electricity. We cannot see this contradiction because we live in financial anxiety; we are constantly, obessively, taking our own financial pulse. Part of every newscast is the state of the stock market at this hour. The result of this is to persuade us, half-consciously, that human reality is money and machines, not nature.

Like other kinds of derangement, the technological culture defends itself in many ways. Its favorite move is to declare that it is, itself, natural. It does this every time it writes its own story in natural metaphors: "a flood of new inventions," we say, forgetting that floods are natural and inventions cultural and deliberate. The French structuralist Roland Barthes remarked some time ago that Western middle-class culture has made history into nature: we see whatever choices we have made in forming our way of life as "the way things are," "the nature of things," even the will of God.

The early pioneers of industrialization believed this quite firmly and explicitly. The first Rockefeller explained his corporate raiding as an example of Darwinian natural selection. "The growth of a large business," he wrote, "is merely the survival of the fittest, the working out of a law of nature and a law of God." In the 95 percent failure rate of business ventures in the 1890s, the great shark of Standard Oil was simply the way things were.

Now the transformation of culture into nature is used to defend technology itself. Since people are natural, the argument goes, anything we do—no matter how it disturbs and damages nonhuman nature—is natural as well. It is one of those enviable arguments that can be used forward or backward. As Christopher Manes says, it can mean "anything we do is natural" or it can mean "nature doesn't really exist, as a category separate from human uses. Why worry?"

This defense of technology sometimes leads, logically enough, to a denial that there is an environmental crisis. Scarcities will be made up by the technological power to turn anything into anything. Do we lack food? Then we will make it out of oil. Do we lack fuel? Then we will make it out of food. On the outer margins of this dream stands the breeder-reactor, which will defy entropy by producing both energy and fuel.

The fallacy of this reasoning is clear: it is really just a kind of sleight of hand. Grain, oil, nuclear ores and whatever you make a reactor out of are all, ultimately, natural materials. They exist in limited supply, and wear out, are exhausted. We cannot transcend this limitation. We cannot, that is, go free of nature. We cannot get a divorce. We can only choose to live with nature in hatred or in love.

Nature Alone (1)

The advocacy of "nature alone" takes place on two levels of sophistication. One is an escape from our dilemma pure and simple; the other is a serious, sympathetic, but probably misleading response to it.

The first level offers no real resistance to the consumer culture. It consumes nature, and breeds and supports commercial complexes of its own. It sees "wilderness" as something to be reserved, not *from* human use, but *for* it—specifically, as an opportunity to get away from the pressures of a culture devoted to making us comfortable. Its cure for the crash of biomes is to fly somewhere where the crash is inaudible, preferably taking along as much civilization as you can carry.

This has been a fashion for a century or more, since bankers and lawyers from New York planted fishing camps in the Adirondacks after the Civil War, and "neurasthenics" like Theodore Roosevelt were sent west to recover. Like all fashions, this one depends on money. This use of wilderness is open only to people who can afford it; it thus widens the division between the prosperous who profit from urban development and can escape it, and the poor who suffer for it and cannot escape it. And, like all fashions, this one comes and goes. In the early eighties, "rough" backpacking in the Rockies was in fashion; since then, requests for permits have dropped by half.

The concept of "unspoiled wilderness" surfaced in the 1880s as an understandable reaction to the spoiling of nature in the slums of Cleveland and Chicago. The concept has had, as one result, the national park and wilderness preservation laws passed in this century. These laws represent a work we need. We need far more wilderness than we have left, and it ought to be far better protected than it is from "public" uses such as logging and grazing. And there is an obvious good in taking people who have had no exposure to wild nature out into even semi-wilderness.

But preserving wilderness and escaping to it are not a solution for the environmental crisis. They are not even an adequate compensation for it.

For one thing, there is a contradiction in the idea of "wilderness preservation." Aldo Leopold stated it most concisely: "all conservation of wildness is self-defeating, for to cherish we must see and fondle, and when enough have seen and fondled, there is no wilderness left to cherish." And of course—under acidified rainfall and showers of ultraviolet—no wilderness is far enough away from us any longer to protect itself. Perhaps the stars are "unspoiled nature." But then we know little about them and cannot get to them to find out.

Nature Alone (2)

The other more deliberate and defensible advocacy of "nature alone" appears in the Deep Ecology movement and its activist allies, such as

Greenpeace and Earth First! These advocates of wilderness begin with love for nature and outrage at its devastation, and both feelings are attractive. The activism they have inspired has often been controversial, but less destructive than irritating.

Earth First!ers are right when they point out the degree to which mainstream conservation groups, such as the Sierra Club, have come to accept the premises of a growth economy. Deep Ecology is right to insist that nature is valuable in and of itself, that it is not given value by human uses for it. A Christian, similarly, is bound by Scripture to affirm that nature has value through the word of the One who made it for his own purposes, which are always to some extent mysterious to human beings.

Following Thoreau and Leopold, Deep Ecologists argue that humans must give up their false dominance over planetary life, and accept an equal "citizenly" place among other natural species. Civilization is so irredeemably anthropocentric—so much a "fake," as Christopher Manes writes—that only an "unmaking" of civilization can save us. We must sink ourselves back into nature in order to stop destroying it.

At this point, however, the Deep Ecologist argument begins to become unworkable, and the scriptural insistence on the uniqueness of humanity among created beings more practical. For we cannot just shuck civilization like an exhausted skin. It is we who pose the danger; and this is because we know our own needs and are able to bend other species to our uses. No germ in its happy destructive business in the blood is (so far as we know) aware of what it is doing.

If we know our own dangerousness, further, we also know, or at least could know, how to make a culture that would preserve the world. Outrage, after all, is a human gift—something we may nobly feel in defense of a redwood, but not something the tree will feel for us.

There is a real and not trivial sense in which we must find our way back to natural good sense along the threads of culture itself. Thomas Hobbes tried to imagine an unmaking of civilization three hundred years ago: "no Culture of the Earth," he wrote in a trance of horror, "no

Navigation . . . no commodious Building . . . no knowledge of the Face of the Earth; no account of Time." But the analysis will not work. Peel all this away and human life vanishes, like an onion. There is no doubt that civilized knowledge has been used to destroy the earth more often than to protect it; and yet how, without "knowledge of the Face of the Earth" or "account of Time," are we to begin a better history?

We cannot live as whales or birds live; we only become more dangerous when we try. Our best efforts, submarines and airplanes, are among the most dangerous things we have ever made. There is an odd sense in which trying to see nature as just an extension of ourselves (as a Deep Ecologist might say) is not very different from insisting that anything we do (as a technological apologist might say) is just an extension of nature. What we must insist on is nature's independence of us—its independent glory as a child of God. The divine plan that includes nature includes, and therefore transcends, us as well.

We are back, then, with the metaphor of marriage. You cannot marry your own foot or your own idea. You marry another creature of God.

The Model of Heaven

Neither nature alone nor culture alone will explain how their marriage is to work; and no separation, short of the collapse of one partner, is possible. We need a further vision, present in both but free of their constraints.

For two centuries we have asked science for this vision. We have thought that an exhaustive scientific description of the planet would tell us not only how to intervene in nature but how far. Governments and corporations greet specific problems, sometimes sincerely, with the cry that we don't yet know enough, that more research needs to be done.

But we will never know "enough." For one thing, we will never know the results of things we haven't yet done. Who thought to ask whether burning coal in Ohio would kill the fish in Maine?

Garrett Hardin says that the crucial environmental question is "And then what?" The wisdom we need must be such as to carry us through an indefinite future series of "And then what?"s; and the fact that we can never give an adequate factual answer to this question means that the wisdom we need will be apart from, and beyond, scientific prediction. This wisdom will have to make it safe for us to be ignorant, as well as safe for us to know.

Christians believe that such wisdom is moral and spiritual, and turn for it first to the Scriptures. We will not find there, and should not expect to find, a complete set of ecological instructions, any more than we expect to find laws for democracy or rules for checkers. What the Scriptures contain is a revelation of God, a record of things he has done and a set of expectations for us accompanied, but not replaced, by provisions for reconciling us with him when we fail.

One of the things God does is to delight in all his works. Another is to entrust some of these to us (who are also his work) for care on the basis of a similar delight.

But the Scriptures are more specific than that. The form of God's delight has a name: it is "wisdom," "the way of God," "the law of the Lord." The crucial thing about this way is that it includes both wonders and rules.

Psalm 19 announces them together: here is the sun that rejoices to run its course, because that is what it was made to do; here are the "statutes of the Lord," and to love and follow them is what we were made to do. The wisdom that set the sun in its way has provided us a way as well, and the two ways are one.

Nevertheless, to human minds they work out differently. They work out as wonders and rules. The way for nature is simply nature itself, guaranteed by the act of God and his partly intelligible reasons. But the way is not solely natural, and culture cannot pick it up by trying to *be* nature. Culture is a response to nature, a rejoinder; it is the amen to nature's prayer. To follow the way as it unfolds in culture is to live so as to preserve nature. But to do this means to live as a human ought to live—that is, according to a moral vision.

It is a mistake, I think, to look for an "environmental ethic" different from the ethics common to human nature-in-nature. A workable environmental ethic means (as Aldo Leopold meant it) extending toward our natural home some of the rights and standards we extend toward other humans; or it means—this might be closer to the sense of Scripture—that to live justly, temperately, gratefully, peacefully, would be to live at home in the creation.

For Christians, and for the West as a whole, the most basic form of this moral vision is the Mosaic code. To help us, the commandments would have to be translatable into sound ecological principles; and many of them are. To honor the parent is to honor memory, the knowledge that ties us to given places and that disciplines innovation. Not to covet is to show a proper respect for what is another's—natural things shared with him or her as well as outright possessions. And it means to show a proper attention to one's own possessions.

The way can also be worked out in routines of practical life, especially when they have a religious meaning. The priestly ritual was understood in Israel to reenact the acts of God in making the world. To be ritually pure, Jacob Neusner says, was to become, in the "holy land," an "incarnation . . . of the model of heaven."

The rules of the Levitical code are not, however, the only practical form the way can take. Nor is the sense of a way unique to Judaism and Christianity. The Scriptures do not claim that it is. The pagans in Romans 1—2 have both the creation and their own consciences for guides.

Nor are the crimes of modern civilization against the way unique to the Christian West, though environmental writers often claim that they are. It is true that the technological culture was born here. We took Eastern inventions, such as gunpowder, and put money and an acquisitive social ethic behind them. But this culture has now been adopted by societies with Islamic, Buddhist, Confucian and animist roots, and it violates their traditional moralities as it does ours. So many traditions speak of a "way" that we may speak, with due caution, of a human consensus.

I am not going to choose one version of "natural law" (for this is also what we are talking about) over another—Aristotle's over Cicero's, Aquinas's over Montesquieu's. We must insist, with the Reformers, that natural law is part of the revelation in Jesus Christ, "the light that lights everyone"; it is not a secondhand grace, a janitor in charge of the cosmos while God is away. But the root doctrine is the same in all places: that a way has been ordained for human life as such, and that to live by it is to be at home on earth.

Of course the technological culture denies that any such way exists. It is an exception to the human consensus. But then that is the point: this is the culture that has denied the way. It has, that is, turned the way against us. The sun still comes forth like a bridegroom; that is its way. But we cannot greet it any longer with joy: we have made it into an enemy.

The Great Convergence

The great danger on the side of the angels, today, is the danger of thinking about the environmental crisis too abstractly. While there is some truth in saying that we need a new "worldview," what we need far more is a new practice. How we work out the *way* in practice is the issue—whether, and how, we make the morality we know effectual. This is what E. F. Schumacher meant when he wrote that we live in the time of "the great convergence," the convergence of "practical sanity and spiritual wisdom." We should be able to see now what was always true, that we must be charitable, peaceable, frugal and patient, and bear each other's burdens, or die.

A culture's effects on the natural environment are not the only test of its adherence to the way. They are one clear test, and perhaps the one most visible and urgent for us. The difficulty is that our machines have put us so far from nature and our own needs that the great convergence is almost invisible to us. We see nature and culture, instead, as morally and spiritually neutral.

"Is there such a thing," Wendell Berry asks, "as a Christian stripmine?" Obviously not. Its damage to the natural world, its expression of greed, dishonesty, waste and callousness make it one of the things you probably cannot do in the strength of Christ.

But our cultural response—and the response of most Christians, who are not thoughtful, as Christians, about their practical lives—has not been to do without stripmines. We do not protest their existence, look after their victims, and turn off our electric corn poppers. We have decided, rather, that stripmines are morally neutral, or that the morality of technology comes solely from how it is used. But there are many inventions that have no good use. What is the good use (as distinct from the good political effect, if any) of a nuclear weapon?

By thinking of machines as morally neutral we empty our practical lives of moral and spiritual dimensions. Cultural affairs become matters of technique and money. Faith becomes harder and harder to carry out the church door: nothing out there seems to have any spiritual point.

"Unbelief is in the air," someone said to me. We can be more concrete than that: unbelief is on all the surfaces of things, in a society where nature exists only to be consumed or made into something else, and cultural objects exist only to be sold. We switch on atheism with the corn popper.

We are engaged, day by day, in a more serious experiment than the quest for a breeder-reactor: we seem to be trying to discover if we can live a spiritual life in a culture of objects that represent no use but sale, no beauty but efficiency, no mystery but technical complexity, no value but their value in dollars; objects that mean only haste, wastefulness, contempt for patience and care. What is the "abundant life" of the gospel if not a drenching of grace that is *both* spiritual and practical? But we live, or are trying to live, half the covenant only: whatever shape our spiritual lives are in, our practice is violently secular. We do not ask ourselves what must become of a spiritual life within such a practice.

In this, as St. Paul might say, we are judged by some parts of the non-Christian world. In Bali, as John Reader writes, "there is no such thing as a secular life. From the Balinese point of view, the entire universe is an expression of enormous spiritual capability." The social result is a complicated network of customs that remind people of their religious lives, and at the same time bind them together for the community effort their agriculture requires. The result of *this* is that the land—small intricately designed paddies and irrigation—is cared for: it produces enough food while each year it gains in fertility.

Bali is a judgment not only of the Christian, or post-Christian, West. China, which has the world's largest intact coal reserves, has announced its intention of doubling its coal consumption by 2000, in the face of the dangers of atmospheric warming. The Confucian Analects forbid harm to neighbors, the complement of the Golden Rule. But the great divergence of spirit and technique has ruled most of the world now for decades.

It is certainly true that Cartesian science and a failing, partial Christianity helped to beget the crises we face. It has been a long time, however, since philosophy or theology set the agenda for practical culture; on the contrary, the evolution of machines and technique, of the power to change the world, sets the agenda for thinking.

It does so by having created and made practical and actable an image of human life that is impossibly wasteful and self-indulgent. Why have federal programs for the aged, Michael Harrington asks, been monopolized by people who, already financially secure, do not need the government's help? There is a political answer: these are people with influence. There is also a cultural answer: these people have seen their opportunity to live the life our whole culture implies. It is leisured, wasteful of resources and of other people's labor, deliberately exploitative, morally neuter—a life of multiple homes, convenience foods, magically green grass, invisible waste. It is the image that lives at the back of our minds, the paradise of the consumer.

Most of us participate in this life to one degree or another. It is not only an image: it is as much a reality as we are able to make it. Thus it has the power to shape the market that supplies all of us; thus it distorts all of our thinking, like an intense electromagnetic field—though, like gravity, it is all but impossible to feel.

To think responsibly about the environmental crisis, then, means to think about the image of desirable human life to which we want to make our everyday lives conform. To think responsibly, as Christians, we will have to judge this image by Christian standards. The danger is not that we will fail to profess the right opinions. The danger is that we will fail, or refuse, to look clearly at our practical lives. The values incarnate *there* are the ones that guide us; they are in fact the ones that we believe.

Plum Island

Against one image, another image. Samuel Sewall wrote this in 1697, about a place in Massachusetts:

> As long as *Plum Island* shall faithfully keep the commanded Post; Notwithstanding all the hectoring Words, and hard Blows of the proud and boisterous Ocean; As long as any Salmon, or Sturgeon shall swim in the streams of *Merrimack;* or any Perch, or Pickeril, in *Crane-Pond;* As long as the Sea-Fowl shall know the Time of their coming . . . As long as Nature shall not grow Old and dote; but shall constantly remember to give the rows of Indian Corn their education, by Pairs; So long shall Christians be born there: and being first made meet, shall from thence be Translated, to be made partakers of the Inheritance of the Saints in Light.

The striking thing about this is how the presence of the gospel, and the promise of redemption, are made real by all of the details of natural fact. Probably Sewall anthropomorphizes more than we are comfortable with: he belonged to a time when this was innocent, when it was still a way of imagining nature and culture living together in charity. But the promise of heaven does not blot out Sewall's devotion to this specific place; to live as one should in this place provides a solid confidence in heaven.

The only mistake Sewall made—it was really no mistake in him, only misplaced confidence—is that he thought nature, self-renewing, self-instructing, would always be a kind of guarantee of Christian hope.

How could nature ever be exhausted, or altered? But we know how.

3
BACKDROP
THINKING

OUT OF SIGHT, OUT OF MIND.

M*y student had called his essay something like "The Wonders of*
Nature." Now, nature *is* a wonder, to my mind; I have often tried to say
so in prose. Still I began to read the essay with some foreboding.

He had taken his bicycle into the country east of Grand Rapids, and
his ride had given the essay a natural logic—first the fading of the suburbs
and the approach of hills and trees; then the road bending along the
river; then the interpretive paragraph, the meditation, about the importance of recognizing the beauties of God's creation.

There was nothing wrong with the plan. Young and healthy, my
students feel sharply what most of us feel, the need to get away from the
convenience of the city. Many writers—Barry Lopez and Mary Austin
and John Muir and Thoreau and Samuel Sewall—have written this kind
of prose with powerful accuracy. And his doctrine was right: the things
that God has made are tense with his presence.

But the essay was in fact full of inaccurate observation, and consequently of false feeling. Its author had written what he had expected to see, not what he had seen or (at least) what was there to see. He had written down the long series of clichés about country roads that city culture had fastened on his eyes.

Without realizing it, he had run into one of our culture's most comprehensive programs—the program against seeing nature or what we do to it. He had not seen that in seven miles of country road there are perhaps one hundred houses but only two working farms and eight or ten vegetable gardens, or a little better than one garden a mile (or fewer than one for every ten families). He had missed the junkyard encrusting both sides of the road for half a mile, the played-out sandpit, the old fields covered with weeds, the rusting corn-cribs and the abandoned farm machinery. He did not mention the empty farmhouses, or the modest trailers in yards full of plaster dwarfs and red cinder mulch that say, at least, that someone is at home.

There is another possible explanation. He may have seen these things and turned resolutely away from them. He was looking for "nature." But nature and culture are married. What he willed to see as empty and virginal has lived with Europeans and Americans for 150 years. The landscape in front of him has a human history.

It was only an accident that he had chosen the road that I live on to write about. My house is one of the hundred, and one of the gardens is mine. I have assigned myself the task of knowing this road; my elderly neighbor, who remembers the road seventy years back, is one of my instructors. I don't want a tourist's knowledge of God's wonders—which is all my student had found.

Giver Houses and Taker Houses

How to read a landscape, how to open its record of natural endowment and historical use, is the concern of academic disciplines such as "landscape history" and "historical geography." These are young disciplines. They began with the work (in England) of W. G. Hoskins, and, in

America, with the postwar essays of John Brinckerhoff Jackson. In the journal he founded, *Landscape,* Jackson showed us that a road might go where it does for political, philosophical, even religious reasons. The history of habitation is really a history of consciousness, in which places and culture shape each other.

One American landscape invention is the "strip," the suburban road with its double file, one building deep, of automobile dealerships, fried-food restaurants, and (now) video shops. It is along such routes that cities invade the countryside. Suburban developments, containing nothing but houses and the occasional church or school, depend on the strip for stores; the road, in turn, breaks ground for developments. Both follow or accompany the establishment of factories and office buildings in "country" settings.

In this way large packages of land are netted into what D. W. Meinig calls the "metropolitan system"—city, suburbs, "engulfed towns," "hamlets . . . farms, and all manner of individual shacks, cottages, mobile homes, houses, and estates" scattered across the countryside. Ten years ago, metropolitan systems had swallowed 27 percent of American landscape.

The suburban infiltration and occupation of the country lie behind the facts of a heavily wooded "country road" like mine. This use of rural land as a setting for urban living has grown quickly in the last decade. In the eighties, tax breaks in the form of deductible mortgage interest made it fashionable to gentrify farmhouses. The new owners normally were not interested in the farms as farms, however, and the farmers, who could not pay the gentrified prices for land, went to the city or ended up on welfare. The social facts of a boom in land prices, therefore, are part of the crisis of agriculture. Fewer than one in ten rural dwellers in the United States today have any connection with a working farm.

It is true that a farm is only one way of living *in* or *with* the landscape. But it is also clear that our typical landscape implies no commitment to the land on the part of landowners, and that most American country-dwellers live *on* or *against* the landscape. They take no further responsibility for it than is implied by a "landscaping" contract with a city firm. The country, that is, is *occupied;* but it is not looked after, or even known. It is the location of the people who live there—their address: but hardly in any significant sense their home.

You can see the result of this on roads even when they run through the countryside far from cities. The small split-level houses are cut on the same pattern in New York or Illinois or Oregon, third-generation descendants of a California original. They stand on shallow lots stamped in the fronts of fields or ex-fields; or in small developments billboarded as "country living," on pans of land that might have been wonderful to plough but are simply naked and hot as settings for houses. As Hans Jenny comments, the virtues that recommend land for ploughing—flatness, good drainage—recommend it equally well for paving.

A friend of mine distinguishes between what she calls "giver" houses and "taker" houses. The "metropolitan system" is made up of taker houses. They are using the air, water, soil and the soil's capacity to produce grass; but they are giving nothing back. The minds of their owners are obviously somewhere else; they have three cars in the driveway, to get somewhere else in, and a boat.

The owners of the giver house have a car too. But their life is bent, to some degree, to contributing to the life of their place. You see it in the vegetable garden, fruit bushes and orchard—perhaps in a barn and livestock. There might be a working windmill, solar panels or a cistern for rain collection. The leaves are not bagged in the fall; they go into the composter. The house is consuming, as it must, some of the place's resources. But the human life in the house is returning to the place, in work, fertility and intelligent care.

Taker houses and their stranded exurban developments are a clear example of what I call "backdrop thinking"—the habit of thinking about nature as a backdrop to human living, not as an ingredient or condition of it. In the theater, a backdrop is the scene, or absence of a scene, in front of which the play occurs. The backdrop is not drawn into the action; no one picks it up or sits down on it. Once you have glanced at it you are free, more or less, to ignore it. Its conception has subordinated it, strictly, to something else.

Backdrop thinking is one of the essential conditions of a consumer society. It is as necessary to consuming as worship is to believing in God. To treat nature as we do, we have had to evolve sophisticated ways of not seeing it even as we look at it. We put nature out of mind, in one way, so that we can consume it in another. Having learned this half-blindness toward nature, moreover, we learned to look at people in the same way, and finally at ourselves.

The Theater of the World

To think about the creation as a theater is an old Western habit. Early maps were often called something like *orbis theatrum,* the theater of the world: the map put the world on display. Shakespeare's playhouse was called the Globe for a similar reason: it put the cultural world on display. A distinguished Renaissance historian has argued that the underside of the Globe's stage roof held a picture of the heavens.

In the *orbis theatrum,* as Jackson reminds us, the play was the work of God. It is not true, as we are so often told, that humankind was at the center of the prescientific universe. In *Paradise Lost,* Raphael tells Adam that the human "dwells not in his own," that we are "lodged in a small partition" of the universe and that "the rest" of it is "ordain'd for uses to [our] Lord best known." For this reason, however—because nature and history were God's continuing invention—the play was worthy of constant, absorbed, detailed watching.

What is playing in the theater of the world now is quite different. The script is human initiative and human fate; we are absorbed in the play of our own doings. The universe is ordained for uses to NASA best known. Paradoxically (you might think), nature gets less attention than it did. We seem to study it carefully. But what we are really studying is the uses we can put it to—that is, we are studying ourselves and our own agenda.

It is not science that is writing this script, but money. This was apparent from the start of the age of technology. Wordsworth understood it: "Getting and spending, we lay waste our powers," he wrote. Getting and spending quickly came to determine the conduct of everything else, society, politics, work, religion. Making money in the capitalist market, further, meant *consuming*. "Little we see in nature that is ours," Wordsworth went on. That makes sense. In a consumer's culture nature is not for possessing, even in a spiritual sense. It exists to be used up.

Throwing Away Your Shoelaces

I doubt whether we think carefully enough about what a "consumer culture" is. It is not, for example, the same thing as a "materialist culture." Just to live, of course, we need an endless parade of things—food, clothing, building materials, music, ideas, human contacts. But the consumer market cannot afford to let us get too attached to anything: consuming is the focus, and if we cherish and preserve a hat, a house or a human contact, we will not consume it. We will not, that is, be back to the market for a new one.

That we come back as often as possible is the deepest of our economic necessities. When lay-offs or a drop in wages discourages us from shopping, the economy goes into shock. But the same shock would be brought on by an outbreak of good workmanship; if we made objects to last the nation would go broke. The heartbeat and blood supply of our culture are to drain the world of resources and have nothing permanent to show for it. Or nothing of value: what we have left overloads landfills and putrifies the air. Waste is an essential piece of economic evidence: it means we are using things up as fast as we can.

But there are two kinds of consuming going on. One is the consumption of objects. The other, more important, consumption pays in a sense no attention to objects. What is being consumed here is the objects' financial identity, their power to occasion an exchange of money. This may be accompanied by the physical consumption of objects—hamburgers are eaten, shoelaces break, cars are smashed—but it need not be. We could just get tired of our shoelaces and throw them away.

We are urged to buy cars on the grounds that driving them, using them up, we will go where we need to go, enjoy ourselves, fulfill our dreams. But the car's utility and glamour are not the objects of our economic attention; they are just the bait. The car is consumed in the way most important to our culture at the moment when we write a check for it, and it passes out of the market.

If this is true, then everything about this culture—economy, manufacturing, ecology, social uses for objects, affections for things—depends on backdrop thinking. We are constantly shoving aside, into the background, the place, the item, the resource, the person that seems to be at the center of action. There is something else more important we have to attend to—the intense little whir of consuming itself.

A Shot of Excitement

How the market keeps us absorbed in consuming was first explained by Karl Marx in a well-known chapter of *Das Kapital*. A commodity, Marx observed, owes very little to the material it is made of or the use we have for it. A table (to use his Platonic example) may be fundamentally wood, or a place to write. On the market, however, it acquires a new self. Now it is a "Shaker-style sofa table" or a " 'Chippendale' console." It has been given a little shot of excitement. It has become something that the market can sell on the market's terms.

We are surrounded, every day, not by things but by the market's images for them; and the images always have a message, not about the things themselves, but about the market. Food is always present, in the advertisement, in uneatable quantity. There is always more toothpaste on the brush in the ad than any set of teeth could warrant. The message is plenty, consumption, the innocent blessedness of having enough to waste.

Some years before *Das Kapital*, Marx had commented that in a capitalist market consumption "creates its object." To look at a manufactured item in terms of its sources, or even in terms of production, would inevitably put some restraint on backdropping: to know what material is best, or how best to make something, is to hold it in mind at least temporarily. But in our economy consumption sets the agenda—which means that the fictive identity advertising gives an object is always more important than the object itself.

But some objects resist such treatment. One is the natural endowment, the thing that was here before we arrived: an oldgrowth forest, the soil's fertility. It can be given a shot of commercial excitement, but the excitement seems more than ordinarily cheap. The forest has its own identity, its own force: this is what "nature" means, that it has a meaning we have not fastened on it, a meaning guaranteed (to a religious mind) by the act of God.

Consumption does not create objects, further, that are valued by the uses, feelings and memories of a coherent body of people. A tribe's hunting territory, a letter in your mother's handwriting, cannot be swapped for cash on even terms. Selling them, when it happens, seems to violate them. There is "something about them" that cannot be reduced to a price. Long human use, reverence and affection protect the "nature" of the thing in the same way nature does.

The identity given an object, therefore, by nature or by the integrity of personal attachment is inevitably contradicted by commercial consumption. To make the object saleable such an identity must be backgrounded; it must be replaced by a sentimental, cartoon image of itself. As for nature, this process has become so automatic that many of us, I suppose, can no longer see in the field or wilderness river *anything* except something to be sold. Between the corporation and the Earth First!er there is a genuine failure of understanding: the executive, his lawyer, perhaps his senator, cannot understand what the conservationist means.

But there is a difficulty at the center of backdrop thinking. This is that consuming itself almost does not exist. The emotions that go with long-term possession are correspondingly long-term; but the psychological instant in which we swap something for money is ephemeral. To be a continued pleasure it must be repeated constantly, just as purchasing has to be repeated constantly to do a consumer economy good. The moment the check is signed the whole transaction ceases to have any particular significance. It is almost as if we could consume everything in sight and pay no attention to anything. We are not getting something for nothing. We are getting nothing for everything.

Backdropping a Place
In *The Control of Nature* (1989) John McPhee exclaims at how people living in the San Gabriel Mountains above Los Angeles "mask out" the authentic danger that their houses will be smashed by debris flows from the slopes above them.

Many things encourage this masking out, including the perennial human capacity to ignore bad news, and the modern belief that all such problems will eventually be solved by a computer. But the most powerful impulse, I think, is backdrop thinking. People live on the San Gabriels not because they wish to know that place, but because it represents commodities—solitude, clean air, a view—that they will pay to consume.

Quite apart from its function as a source of subsistence, nature has become a commodity with us. It is the largest and most significant thing that has been assigned a market identity. It appears on billboards to help sell beer and cigarettes. It plays a supporting role in sports programs whose sponsors sell skis, breakfast cereal and rooms in Hawaiian hotels. It sells condominiums in Vermont. It is for sale directly in exurbia, as a country setting for homes.

Of these examples the last is the most interesting; it illustrates how instinctive and complicated backdrop thinking has become. The false identity the real estate market puts on nature is simply—"nature." This is what we call it. "Nature" sells the lot. Yet the place's natural facts—streams, grasses, wildflowers, rocks, trees, topsoil—are ruthlessly ignored. The developer will destroy any or all of them to produce a standardized setting for a standard house, to be sold to consumers who have (as we say) "better things to do" than to look after the place they have bought. The place must be rendered blank, so that it may be made into a suitable "natural" setting.

The house that is built there may set nature at defiance. Driving through north Texas a few summers ago, I saw a development of Cape Codders sprawled across a treeless hilltop. Now it is a natural fact that the Texas summer sun is blistering, and a sensible conclusion that to expose a frame house on a naked hill is to subject it to furious heat. But the developer had made his contempt for these facts obvious; and the basis of his contempt was confidence that there would always be enough energy to supply every room with its own air conditioner.

Does it make sense to call these houses "unnatural"? Is there such a thing as a "natural" house? I asked after indigenous forms of architecture; my students, all Texans, had no idea. I had an *idea*, at least, and I half expected my Hispanic students to come up with it: the thick-walled, courtyarded houses preserved for tourists to see in San Antonio. Such houses were sensible, ingenious and cool; they took nature into account, even into partnership, exhausted no fossil fuel, expressed cultural tact. They were like hundreds of examples, before this century, of what John S. Taylor calls "commonsense architecture."

But isn't the life to be lived in a "country" setting more "natural" than life in the city? That depends. It is certainly true that giver houses are easier to establish where there is ground for gardens and a woodlot for fuel. Most of the houses even in the country, however, are taker houses. Whatever "country" means to their owners, it is not a commitment to nurturing the health of their place.

Actually, we know what *country* means. It is the commercial setting for a "country lifestyle"—landscaping by the lawncare company, morning jogs with Walkman and sauna afterwards, the membership at the health club, the diet dinner, the check to the Sierra Club. Now, comfort is not a vice; and it is clearly better to jog than to die. The difficulty is that the country lifestyle has been made in the image of, and for the profit of, the consumer economy that provides its goods and services. As far as nature itself is concerned, this life is a form of blindness.

As for the check to the Sierra Club: the country lifestyle may be the basis, the horizon, of practical decisions about country on a larger scale. And we are not prepared to make sound decisions about wilderness by our image of nature as unbroken green lawn and a hypertrophied bed of geraniums. Here, once again, the consumer image is standing in our way.

Invisible Gardeners
Few of us will ever see true wilderness, even supposing it survives this century of consuming. On the whole, it may be desirable that few of us should see it. And yet the life of nature is all around us, where we least expect to find it; and the skills we would need to free it from its commodity image are available. "What is a course of history, or philosophy, or poetry," wrote Thoreau, "compared with the discipline of looking always at what is to be seen?" What the consumer culture has made a backdrop, we can bring back into thought and into the reach of conscience.

I use the word *conscience* because learning to see nature once again is not merely an aesthetic opportunity. It is a moral and spiritual duty, a debt we owe to nature's Maker. This is the more true because no culture can make nature into a backdrop without doing the same to people. The "invisibility" of the American poor, which Michael Harrington has called more than once to our attention, is in part a result of the same mental dodges that hide clearcut forests.

Nature and culture are married primarily by necessity: culture can exist nowhere but inside nature, and it needs what nature provides. The connection, moreover, is made by necessary work; and there must always be people to do it. As it denies nature, then, or turns it into calendar pictures and lifestyles, the consumer culture must deny the people who do "natural work."

In his classic study of British village life, *Akenfield* (1969), Ronald Blythe recorded the memories of people who did manual labor in and around aristocratic "big houses." A maid meeting a house guest in the hall was expected to turn and face the wall until the guest had passed; she was to make herself part of the furniture, so that the guest would not have to cope with her being human. The gardeners had to finish their work in early morning, so that the lady of the manor would never see them and the gardens would seem to flourish on their own. This was a lie about nature and culture at the same time. If the gardeners were invisible, their sophisticated traditional knowledge of gardens was invisible as well.

In slave-owning societies it was the slave who farmed, cooked, washed, built, tore down, disposed of waste—who did the labor that intervenes between nature and culture. But any of us who buys a quart of Californian or Mexican strawberries is in danger of standing in the slave owner's position, though no one has a deed for the slave. Someone has done our dirty work for us. It can be very dirty work. It is done by people such as migrant laborers, who are in such straits that they cannot refuse to do the work everyone else refuses to do.

We may feel some anxiety about them; we may have boycotted lettuce in support of César Chavez. But backdropping people is more than ignoring them. It is the process of transforming them into commodity images. Consider, for example, the familiar happy Colombian coffee-grower. He represents—that is, he conceals—whole classes of people dislodged from their own farms to work for American specialty food markets. He represents the power of the American economy in smaller economies, which forces their land and food-provision systems to serve ours. This contradicts the best American intentions. We meant to build a society free of the feudalities of the past. In fact, we have extended the feudal system from classes to nations. Whole populations face the wall as we pass.

But we backdrop other Americans as well. A bland phrase such as "the growth of service industries" conceals the employment of millions of people, at or near minimum wage, to do the subsistence work of society. The fast-food industry profits from classes of invisible labor—teens, minorities, the disabled—who cannot afford not to take the work. "The contrast between the electrical engineer and the dishwasher," Harrington writes, is "one aspect of the new poverty." Our hopes for economic expansion, that is, focus on one kind of work and not another—on the high-tech jobs that, through the labor-saving effects of technological innovation, are always growing fewer.

My point is not, of course, that no one should do subsistence work. Someone must always do it; it is necessary work, a good deal more necessary to a healthy culture than the writing of this book. We must face this, both to make sure that the work is done in the best way and to protect the people who do it. The backdrop principle allows us to punish people for doing work all of us depend on; it allows us to put the natural sources of culture so far out of mind that we fail to see what this work, done badly, costs the planet.

One of the motives behind the Industrial Revolution was simply a desire to escape the driving necessity of subsistence labor. The thought was that building machines to do this work—making the machine a slave—would liberate people. It was a vision Marx, for one, inherited from the first generation of inventors.

There is no doubt that in a narrow sense this has happened. It was easier to combine wheat than to scythe it, rake it and thresh it with a flail. But this narrow sense is very narrow. It leaves out the social effects of the combine (usually assumed to be positive, but surely not universally so), and what the entire transformation of farming has meant for the field.

For it may be that there is no such thing as "labor-saving"—only "labor-deferring." Ruth Cowan has argued that even the indoor domestic labor-saving devices of the twenties—the vacuum sweeper and refrigerator—did not in fact save labor. They only saved paid labor (that is, they put the maid out of work) and placed the burden of subsistence work on the housewife herself.

But another deferral, more profound, was going on at the same time. For the refrigerator, the food-processing system behind the supermarket and the car with which subsistence errands were eventually to be run all defer labor to natural energies—which has meant, since the electrification of the industrial world and the proliferation of cars, to all of the resources we have burned to run our machines. And this is the burning that has raised the atmosphere's temperature. Of course, we cannot see the carbon in the air either.

Mining Yourself
The final step in this process is the most bizarre, and yet (to a culture such as ours) the most necessary. You cannot think about the creation and other people as backdrops to consumption without thinking of yourself in the same way.

It seems bizarre to say this because our moral judgment on the consumer culture is that it depends on selfishness. This is normally why we object to it, when we do. The advertiser's appeal is always to *my* pleasure and profit. And if I think of everything in the world as a backdrop to the intensity and felicity of my own experience, then I will have narrowed my attention to myself. Indeed, I will be alone with myself. There is no company in the kingdom of consuming.

That loneliness is the inevitable consequence of gobbling everything in sight is so obvious that the consumer culture itself has taken note. One of the subtler turns in our popular ethics recently has been the emergence of an ethic of self-cultivation as an alternative to "materialism" or "consumerism." We cultivate ourselves by attending to health and psychological wholeness, choosing a "simple lifestyle," learning something about painting or Shaker design, taking up Zen exercises, meditation or channeling. "My neighbors are into nature," one of my students told me. "They jog every morning."

Now there is sense in choosing exercise over another soap opera (though if you jog on an exercise machine in the health club you may not have to choose). The difficulty is that none of this constitutes an alternative to consumerism. The corporations that provide consumer goods do not care whether we buy televisions or not as long as we buy something; it is the buying that is crucial; the object we buy can be backdropped. As long as the market is allowed to provide the machines and energy for the health club or the car to drive to the meditation session, the system will be intact.

As long as self-cultivation specializes in lifestyles purchasable on the market, then, it is no real alternative to the selfishness of consuming. Nor is it any protection, ultimately, against consuming ourselves. For its main consumables are not objects but experiences, states of consciousness. It appeals less to physical appetite than to emotional and spiritual appetite; not to the taste in your mouth but to the flavor of a metaphysic or the aroma of a worldview.

The same rules apply to consuming experiences as apply to consuming objects. There is the same requirement that in order to keep consuming we must move as quickly as possible from purchase to purchase—from experience to experience, that is, in the same way that we move from car to car or from software package to software package. There is the same demand for novelty, and the same necessary refusal of any lasting commitment. Self-cultivation means being a tourist of yourself. "Wherever you are" is a temporary location. It is a duty to make sure that you are not tied down by things—education, a vocation, a marriage, a faith—that are designed to tie you down.

In this context it seems less psychologically inconceivable to backdrop yourself: "you" are only the setting for experiences. But that is only half of the process. As with a place or a migrant worker, the thing that is backdropped is consumed.

Here we come up against something that, again, seems inconceivable: how can you consume a self? A Christian understanding of human being would suggest that in the end it is impossible. The human self exists, finally, in God's awareness of it. Body and mind, like male and female, are dimensions of human being, not resources, equipment or acquisitions. You cannot *make use of* your body and mind; you *are* your body and mind.

Yet we do talk plainly, and with surprising casualness, as if human selves were just resources. The present rhetoric of education puts the student in these terms. The publicity from the admissions department tells the student that the college will help her to *discover, develop* and *market* her *potential,* as if she were not a child of God and a citizen of humanity, not an end (as Kant would say) in herself, but a deposit of ore to be mined and consumed (paradoxically) for her own profit. To do this, even with the student's consent, is to commit the kind of hateful standardized violence that characterizes the consumer market in all of its phases.

That the student tries to do, and suffer, this in cooperation with one cultural institution and in service to another—preparing herself in school to put herself on the market—makes the real meaning of the process clear. It turns out, in reality, to be something quite different from consuming yourself—that is, from profiting from the consumption of yourself. It means turning yourself over to the consumer market. *It* will assay, mine and manufacture you, place you or move you, supply experiences and in all of this make you a highly efficient instrument for generating the exchange of money. You will not be allowed to settle down or settle in, to know or look after yourself, to commit yourself, finally, to any person or Person. You will not be your own. You will have become a resource; and the market will not hesitate to consume you.

4
GOOD
GIFTS

I BOUGHT AN UNCTION
FROM A MOUNTEBANK.

WILLIAM SHAKESPEARE

I *flew into Detroit in the late afternoon. It had been a day of defiances* and surrenders, liftoffs and landings, ups and downs. I was going home in a series of abortive leaps. Despite the speed of the planes, I felt restless and resentful—the convenience of modern travel has not abolished distance, only effort and hope and curiosity—and I wandered down the long gateway corridor for no good reason except to avoid the comfort of the flight lounge.

But there was the Paradies Gift Shoppe. (Always the double *p* and an *e*.) Paradise indeed, I thought, and went in; I needed to buy something for my children—a gift, a substitute me, a sign of love despite absence, an evidence of travel, like the leaf of Noah's dove. Nothing there so green and hopeful as a leaf. There were hot glass cabinets full of jewelry, wire racks with tangles of chains and earrings, teddy bears and teddy ducks like bins of polyester fluff.

The rack of "fancy foods": that meant chocolate, bags of snack nuts, and wallets of pastry fat with syrup. The rack of magazines—candied bodies and stares of hatred beneath the lacquered hair—beside the rack of novels: reveries for the afternoons of modern travel, one sexual reference per page, so that your hormones speed up and slow, speed up and slow, as the planes lift and fall. A plastic jeep crawled in its carpeted box, flipping over at each wall to scuttle back, whining, back and forth.

I stood in the shop and felt despair, unable after a moment to distinguish among the kinds of trash for sale. The most innocuous things—T-shirts stiff with graphics of the Motor City—cost more than I could spend. The cheapest items—the squamous extruded-plastic monsters; Blue Mouth Tricks, "make your teeth and tongue turn blue"—were simply ugly and stupid.

Four or five of the shops stood in a line, and I walked in and out of each. Once we had learned to backdrop nature, once we had made the culture of consuming our pattern, our ideal, this is what we came to—identical shops full of "goods" with no goodness in them but temporary amusement and extortionate profit.

I walked in and out of the shops, unable to stand still. Everything in them was the same, desperately, grotesquely itself; had been that way from the instant the heat mold had squeezed it out; nothing about it would ever change, it would never grow or ripen or reproduce or decay; it would pass into the earth as a bit of unassimilable junk, a plastic bone in the living throat. I walked from paradise to paradise, and the stuff on the shelves pretended to be heaven and sank into hell, and eventually I bought something and went out to catch my plane.

The Glory of Him Who Moves All Things

We learn the life of faith by analogy; there is no other way. A phrase like "God loves me" would be like $E=mc^2$, a chain of unimaginables, except that I know what love is from human love, God's love from the love of friends and wife and parents and children. We comprehend care by caring and being cared for.

I know what a good gift is. The carafe at my elbow, with this chapter's coffee in it, the pen with which I am working these sentences over, were both gifts. The gray sunlight (it is winter) flowing over the paper is a sheer gift; there is nothing I could do to earn it, or to repay the debt I owe for waking, every morning since my birth, to see the light around me. It is one of the kinds of light in which I see light.

But the window light is a different sort of gift from the pen in my hand. Sometimes, when the church is troubled by pantheism and pursues the *via negativa*, we insist that sunlight is just an analogy of the light in which God dwells. When someone quotes, "Let us walk in the 'light' as he is in the 'light,' " you can almost hear the quotation marks. Sometimes, on the other hand, when the church is more concerned with secularity, we insist that the earthly light is an example of, a reflection of, heavenly light. This is how Dante saw it: "La gloria di colui che tutto muove / Per l'universo penetre e risplende"—"The glory of Him who moves all things rays forth / Through all the universe, and is reflected."

In either case, however, human gifts are more problematic. We seldom see a human act so selfless and transparent to goodness that it seems to be an immediate expression of God's grace, and not just a reference to it. Humanity, as Herbert said, "is a brittle crazie glass." Most of the time we block out more light than we let through.

Which is something to be repented of, of course, but also an opportunity, a set of conditions for work. We might say that the work of culture is to find ways of living that are as transparent to grace as possible—that distort as little as possible "the glory of Him who moves all things," whether this glory appears in nature or in the more ambiguous form of human action.

Sometimes, looking through the history of cultures, you seem to see one: a way of living in which people flourish without greed, human skill grows without arrogance and the earth abounds. Some of the medieval monasteries, for instance, like Saint-Gall, whose scriptorium turned out beautiful manuscripts, and whose dead were buried among the trees of the orchard. This is what the dream of the American family farm has meant— sufficiency and consolation. Something like this is the meaning of the "small, rational, beautiful, and durable towns . . . centered about the Church" that Edward Abbey found in the Mormon Southwest. This is so clearly what we have *not* made of our culture as a whole, however, that we normally invoke these images only to reject them, defensively, as dreams.

The importance, the necessity, of the work of culture is in part what the incarnation meant. If the Word had come merely to die, his life could have been shorter. He came, however, to live with us as well as to die for us. "Are the consequences of Christ's life more important than His life?" Kierkegaard asked. The answer is clearly no. The consequences depend on the life; and to live with us meant accumulating years and experience, taking up a vocation, paying taxes, going to weddings. It meant participating in a given culture. And it is Jesus' life among us that implies a practical criterion for our life: what if we thought of the culture we are building as a place for him to live?

For the incarnation puts an intense pressure of significance on the familiar stages and institutions of human existence—the natural birth of a human mother, the long years in a manual trade, the baptism among friends, the marriage feast. We always knew these things; they were always the human occupations and preoccupations. With the incarna- tion they became, also, the medium in which we are to enact the mystery of God's love for us.

But then we must enact it. There is the catch. The mystery has come to rest in the normal human action: suddenly it, the action, is the crux of the matter. If we act selfishly, manipulatively, toward each other, we must not hope to understand how Christ acts toward the church. The mystery will be invisible to us. We will have thrust it away along with the care and courtesy we refused to show. We will be standing in the way of the light.

Similarly, we will be blocking out light when we build a material and economic life that centers around the Paradies Gift Shoppe. I thought of the reason for this while I stood there, and it followed me out to the plane, pounding in my ears: "If you, who are evil, know how to give good gifts to your children, how much more will your heavenly Father give the Holy Spirit to those who ask!"

Turning Out the Lights

The urgency of that analogy is intense. It is in part a reassurance—"if you know, then you may be sure God knows"—but weighting that is an enormous responsibility—"if you forget, or refuse to know, then how will you be sure . . ."

I had no doubt of the evil we are capable of. I had been looking in the face of our common culture, and it was dirty, trivial, sniggering and inane. The evil had tainted the gifts, or produced them in its own image. Standing there, I did not know where to find a good gift; with the possibilities at hand, I did not know how to *give* one. Where was I to find evidence in that place that God had given us the Holy Spirit?

I could have comforted myself that I did not mean to give a bad gift, and that my children would welcome what I brought in the warm light of my intention. "It's the thought that counts": thoughtless and mercenary people are always saying this to us, and then revealing their hypocrisy by urging us to buy whatever they are selling as a way of showing our good intentions. But the degradation of the gift shop held me back. What sort of intentions would its gifts express?

The gifts would have said, I think, that I did not much care what my children needed, that I was willing to give them trivia and degradation, that I did not really think them worth any more. But beginning with that, how would they struggle back to the confidence that their heavenly Father thought them worth infinitely more?

For the one in some obvious ways depends on the other—the confidence in God on the state of the world. "If I tell you of earthly things and you do not believe, how shall you believe if I tell you of heavenly?" What we do with "earthly things," then, we can expect to have some effect on our sense of "heavenly." We may have thought that the physical effects of the environmental crisis—the genocide of species, the dismantling of the atmosphere—were the worst we would have to face. I do not think they are.

For we ought to consider that the fouling of the earth and the degradation of human culture might make it impossible for us to imagine (and therefore to believe) that God cares for us. If our assurance of the gift of the Holy Spirit depends on our own capacity to give good gifts, we are in a desperate state. It is hard, now, to give a good gift. It is like trying to pronounce love in a language made up of curses.

What could be clearer evidence of our condition than a store full of presents? The Paradies Gift Shoppe is the heaven of our minds in this era. Its wares are prototypical products of modern industry, arrogant toward nature, servile toward money, insulting to human skill. They destroy health, contentment and clarity of mind, and replace them with illness, restlessness and stupidity.

After a few minutes in the Shoppe you can no longer tell if anything there has its right price, or compare one thing with another. There is no standard for comparison because nothing there has any real value. The food would be unhealthy to eat, the writing unhealthy to read; the toys are crude and dull, the adornments ugly. I, an ordinary human father, full of love, found it all but impossible to buy something that would not insult my children's intelligence or harm their bodies.

It is an article of the church's faith that natural and cultural goodness is a fruit of the Spirit's presence in the world. We are surrounded by daily evidence of the Spirit's energy and of the sureness of the Spirit's order.

But this does not mean that we always see them. The revelation, which is in itself a good and perfect gift, has chosen to come to us in alterable circumstances, in forms that we can change or deface. What happens when a culture turns away, not only from the gospel, but from the natural world, and from its own proper goodness as well—when it comes to desire the flimsy, the grotesque and the moronic over the well-made, the fruitful and the worthwhile? How far can such a transformation *down* proceed before a culture simply goes out, like a light, and we are left without a medium through which to imagine the gifts of the Spirit?

We Are Not Materialists

It has been, all of my life, one of the themes of evangelistic preaching that Americans are "materialistic." Needless to say, there is some point to this. As much as anything, the last two centuries of life in the industrial Northwest of the world are defined by our having gained enormous power over the material conditions of living. We have gained this not only by technical ingenuity, but by choosing material welfare as the goal of society's efforts. Where the ancients built cities (as Aristotle says) to train us in moral excellence, we have built corporations to extract coal, produce more toasters and postpone physical death. No doubt all of this does interfere with the life of faith.

Yet for all of the preaching, American evangelical Christianity is sunk as deeply as any social bloc in the consumer culture—more deeply than some. There are many reasons for this. One is that we do not see how deep the problem goes. Hedonism, which we are always deploring in the abstract, is an economic necessity, as Keynes and Galbraith explained to us, because it stimulates production. Sermons against material gratification seldom get very far, because if we were moderate in our pleasures we would probably lose our jobs.

We do not really see, moreover, how close the problem comes. We can sit through a sermon on greed and waste in untroubled serenity, because no one points out to us that the ordinary suburban house, the taker house, is greedy and wasteful in design.

But preaching against materialism fails, mostly, because it is too simply and exclusively negative. We damn without even faint praise.

And what we fail to praise is the true, necessary materialism of human life. We entangle our morality, therefore, with a kind of nonsense: we seem to think that we can cure materialism by having nothing to do with matter at all.

But we are material creatures. What will we eat if not a material tomato? To refuse to think materialistically is not to cure ourselves of greed; it is to turn over most of our daily lives to the consumer market. This means turning over the material world—made and delighted in by the God we profess to praise—to the devastation implied by clearcut watersheds and toxic waste dumps. A bad materialism, then, grows up in the absence of a good materialism. The only way to cure an unhealthy materialism is to learn a healthy one.

We Are Materialists
The first step in this would be to readmit to our minds the facts of biological necessity: that to live in peace in the world where we have been placed, we need food, warmth and shelter, and that if we are going to have these for long, we must find them in a way that does not destroy the earth's capacity to supply them. To make food, warmth and shelter the responsibility of machines and multinationals is to guarantee this destruction. Therefore we must take our own material lives back into our own hands.

What would a true materialism be like? First, it would be moderate. It would not put such pressure on the world, or on ourselves, as to destroy either one. This is not an exclusively Christian lesson. The Buddhist principle of "right livelihood" teaches that enough to sustain life is enough, and that more involves us wrongly in the world of desire. For Christians the lesson is more complicated. We believe in the goodness of the created world; our moderation must flow from gratitude, and from a refusal to make our lives a burden to other creatures.

A true materialist—one who loved objects and desired, naturally, to live among them—would want them to last. A truly materialist culture would make its everyday possessions, its forks and tables and paper, so that they would last. It would be a matter of pride that you had owned the same chair or house for forty years, or the same books all of your life.

The objects in a consumer culture, as we said in chapter three, must not last. We cannot afford, financially, to have them last. They must entice us and then bore us or fail us. They must be flashy but not beautiful, complicated but dull; they must wear out quickly. They must be as little likely as possible to attract affection. What does that Styrofoam cup at your elbow mean to you? You will throw it away in a moment.

In a true materialism, things would be beautiful, personal and significant. Everything would have a personal association connected with it, or a story, or a religious idea. Good work could be required of everyone, and every kind of work would show the same virtues—moderation in scale, the worker's respect for materials, shared standards of value and therefore just evaluation. Everyone in such a culture could "[make] use of things that are made artfully . . . and everyone [would possess] an art of some sort, whether of painting, sculpture, blacksmithing, weaving, cookery, or agriculture"—or teaching, writing, engineering or selling.

The Picasso in the Subway

The author of that quotation, Ananda Coomaraswamy, wrote once that art is "a conscience about form." He did not mean that conscience is merely aesthetic, but that the standards for art, and for good work of any kind, are set by conscience—that is, by a larger spiritual vision. In the technological culture, the standards for work are set by money, efficiency and power. The objects we live among evince no human quality but technical intelligence. They mean nothing but that technical power is supreme. They tell us nothing about nature except that it has been reduced to an invisible, neuter "stuff" that we can use, waste or destroy at will.

To see work as an evidence of conscience is not to see it as a means of salvation—the attitude we associate, perhaps unfairly, with people who want to redeem society by hanging Rembrandt and Picasso reproductions in the subway. Coomaraswamy understood that art of this kind has been "abstracted from the general activity of making things for human use," and that such an abstraction makes the art snobbish and useless while it debases "things for human use" into machine-made trivia. The reproductions in the subway will not help much. They only emphasize the tawdriness of the other objects there.

The traditional cultures that Coomaraswamy studied saw things the other way around: not salvation *by* art, but the salvation *of* art (and of shoes and storage pots) by making it the medium of something more important, of piety, justice and the knowledge of God. Not that the storage pot has a moral pasted on it; this would violate the excellence of storage pot design. But it might be immediate evidence, an incarnation, of a moral discipline in the potter that signified his or her understanding of a place in creation.

The Welsh painter and poet David Jones observed that even the bread and wine of Communion are cultural things. Grain is natural, bread is an artifact. "Something has to be made by us," Jones wrote, "before it can become for us his sign who made us."

But the principle stretches further than that. Our capacity for making things is part of the image of God in us—the crucial part, according to Dorothy L. Sayers. What this means is that we, like God, are continually making little images of ourselves; and this making either reflects our debt to God, by being the kind of work he would do, or it doesn't. Either we do good work in sound and beautiful forms, work that respects the nature it is made of—or we make trash in stupid forms, that destroys the character of its natural precedent and accumulates in a wall of junk between us and the creation. Either way, we build a cultural world full of spiritual clues. But in good work the clues are all of the love of God; in bad, all of human presumption.

The Church in a Culture of Trash

The point, I repeat, is not that fine pottery and paintings will save our souls. Coomaraswamy, though not a Christian, understood this clearly. The piece of fine work will teach us, as he said, about God. But the vision that shapes it is religious, not aesthetic, to begin with. It is revelation; it is the gift of grace.

The question, then, is not how we are saved, but how we work out our salvation. I wrote in chapter two that we seem to be trying an experiment: we seem to be wondering if we can live moral and spiritual lives—peaceable, patient, temperate, self-controlled lives, to use the checklist in Galatians—in a world where no object suggests or embodies such virtues.

We might think we had the same chance as any culture of running into patient and humble people. But do we? Is patience, in fact, likely to find its quiet blossoming in a culture of mass production for mass consumption—a culture in which nothing lasts, nothing needs to be preserved, tolerated or worked with, because everything can be thrown away and replaced, nothing ever has to be made because everything has been prefabricated?

Of course every church has someone in it whose goodness it would be stingy to doubt. And there is always the chance of heroic sanctity. But a culture cannot be judged by its heroes and great works. It must be judged by its ordinary people and ordinary products; and the normal products of our economy hardly encourage anything like the virtues we profess to desire.

It is not patience that is a virtue with us, but impatience. A market based on stimulated consumption must get on to the new product as quickly as possible; the economics of sales depends on "moving the goods." All of the gifts of this culture must be temporary, or the economy withers. All of its satisfactions must be temporary, and brief.

Our restlessness shows up in other things as well. We demand, with terrible impatience, that marriage satisfy us immediately and completely, or at least that we be allowed to escape from it immediately if it does not. But how can a church that endorses the culture of trash ask for good work—patient, humble, devoted work—in human relationships? The answer is that the church does not. Like the market, the church wants a quick technical solution—a pill for marriages, a new pitch for the gospel.

A church that participates in a culture of trash, then, is put under terrible strain. The very objects it uses, the medium of its human life and mission, mean things that the church cannot possibly accept and remain faithful to its gospel.

The church shares the humility of the incarnation. Like its Master, it is subjected to the forms of ordinary cultural life. The ways in which people work, eat, buy, sell, invent, make and remember are the ways in which the church works out its salvation. They show (or do not show) the church's good health. They are its fruits, its flesh and bone, its witness.

Perhaps the most discouraging thought, then, is the suspicion that most American church members would have felt more or less at home in the Paradies Gift Shoppe. But there is a sense, real and not fanciful, in which we have to choose between the paradise of consumption and the kingdom of God. The more at home in the second, I think, the less at home in the first. And where we feel at home is crucial: in the kingdom's practice, the spiritual waits on the cultural, the invisible on the visible. And it is the cultural and the visible that we have been given responsibility to shape.

5
The
BREAKING
of
NATIONS

I*n December 1799, Dorothy and William Wordsworth, orphan sister* and brother, moved from southwest England to Dove Cottage, near Grasmere, in the Lake District. They had long planned and wished to find a home they could maintain on William's small invested income—a home close to a rural culture and to the mountains that they both loved.

A modern mind cannot help being moved by this event, this moment. It was as momentous, in its way, as industrialization itself, because it exemplified, so early on, one of our typical responses to industrialization—the withdrawal from its destructions; the hope of finding a renewed spirituality in nature. What came after the move to Grasmere was Thoreau on Walden Pond, John Muir in the Sierras, homesteading in Alaska and Deep Ecology.

Dorothy and William were both writers. William was writing the poems that expressed that new, half-Christian spirituality we call Romanticism. Dorothy began, in May 1800, to keep a journal that runs, in the fragments we have, through January 1803. The "Grasmere Journals" are an example of great personal prose; they have the power to give us the feel of being alive in a particular time and place. In this vein of writing there have been essayists (Montaigne), letter-writers (Dorothy Osborne, Horace Walpole) and diarists (Pepys, Parson Woodforde, Boswell)—none more lucid, selfless and imaginatively powerful than Dorothy.

One constant of the journals is the procession of beggars past Dove Cottage. Dorothy's first entry (for May 14) closes:

A young woman begged at the door—she had come from Manchester on Sunday morn with two shillings and a slip of paper which she supposed a Bank note—it was a cheat. She had buried her husband and three children within a year and a half—all in one grave—burying very dear [expensive]—paupers all put in one place . . .

It goes on like this for the whole thirty months of the journals. What Dorothy was recording (though she herself could only look for causes) was another crucial fact about modern life—that it creates and feeds on the constant disorientation of people. Dorothy lived, wanted to live, in an established community. The industrial culture has always destroyed these communities wherever it found them.

The beggars in Grasmere were the fringe of an enormous demographic unsettling, in which hundreds of thousands of people were dispossessed of their inherited places and funneled in hit-or-miss fashion toward the industrial cities. Neither the industries for which these people became a "labor force" nor the day's social planning was prepared to deal with them in anything but hit-or-miss fashion. Anyway, there were advantages in confusion: it meant that the mill owners, banks and urban builders could do very much what they pleased—could act, that is, according to what they were coming to see as another "law of nature," the law of the freedom of capital, the law of laissez-faire commerce.

The human pain this new law implied was not, of course, entered in the mill accounts. It was hidden by the "naturalness," the apparent unstoppability, of industrialization itself; also by the rationalization, made explicit in the 1830s, that all of this agony was justified by benefits to the rest of society. That this "one-should-die-for-the-good-of-the-people" reasoning—what we might call the Caiaphas argument—has serious moral and practical flaws was not much considered. But there were always witnesses to the suffering. Dorothy's journals, in this dimension of them, join the writing of William Cobbett and Harriet Martineau in a line that runs through Engels and Ruskin to Harry Caudill and Wendell Berry.

Green Fields, Neighbors

Dorothy's entry for Wednesday, September 3, 1800, records the funeral of a woman who, without family, was "buried by the parish." It is wonderfully written, without affectation and full of joy. What it rejoices in is the competence of the "parish" to acknowledge and dignify the pauper's death.

The coffin was neatly lettered and painted black and covered with a decent cloth. They set the corpse down at the door and while we stood within the threshold the men with their hats off sang with decent and solemn countenance a verse of a funeral psalm. The corpse was then borne down the hill and they sang till they had got past the Town-end. I was affected to tears while we stood in the house, the coffin lying before me. There were no near kindred, no children. When we got out of the dark house the sun was shining and the prospect looked so divinely beautiful as I never saw it. It seemed more sacred than I had ever seen it, and yet more allied to human life. The green fields, neighbours of the churchyard, were as green as possible. . . . I thought she was going to a quiet spot.

The entry's consolation arises from a sense of community. Dorothy records here the "alliances" that surrounded the death even of a solitary ("no near kindred"). The entry offers a kind of definition of community:

it is what holds people together by the strength of "common things." This community is their resilience in the face of death; its evidence is their instinctive propriety, their confidence about what ought to be done. The parish and the funeral are Christian, and yet the people have a kind of spiritual independence: the only religious rite Dorothy records, the one that fits the situation, is the psalm the people sing (Dorothy had seen the local priest "half-drunk the day before in a pot-house").

But the community extends beyond its people. This extension gives it what we would call an ecological significance. The fields are the "neighbours of the churchyard" because the people work in the one and rest in the other. The places are neighbors as the people are, and the people are neighbors of their places.

Dorothy was less aware, I think, of the strains between Christianity and Romantic naturalism than William and their mutual friend Samuel Taylor Coleridge were later to be. What moves her to tears is the closeness of the sacred to the domestic. Neighborliness domesticates the mystery; it brings it home. The dead woman is at home in death as in life, in a "quiet spot" within the community of people and land.

The Great Transformation
The tradition of writing that recorded the coming of industrialization is full, too, of pictures of community. This is because the nature and meaning of industrialization were felt most clearly where it collided with settled, traditional agricultural communities—the kind of community that today persists, mostly marginally, in Africa and Asia. In 1750 most people lived in such communities. In order to succeed, however, industrialization needed the cooperation, or at least the conformity, of most people. Therefore it had to change the kind of life they were living.

The popular history of the Industrial Revolution sees it as essentially scientific and financial, something that arrived quickly and inevitably as machines were invented and capital accumulated. But such an event must have, or make for itself, a social opportunity. It does not happen in a vacuum. There was a way of life in place, on the ground, when the revolution began; and this way had to be destroyed (not "transcended" or "improved upon") before industrial culture could come into its own. Karl Polanyi stated the reasons for this destruction in *The Great Transformation* (1944), his classic study of the coming of industrial Europe. Polanyi saw the necessary animosity of the capitalist market to traditional societies. The market "liquidated" them, "smashed them up," to use Polanyi's phrases, in order to create a "free" social arena in which people could be forced to sell labor to buy what they needed.

The trouble with traditional communities is that they offer too many securities. No one starves, because everyone has a right to share the crop or hunt, however poor; no one lives or dies alone (not even elderly paupers), because life is lived in the clan or parish. You cannot buy such securities; they have nothing to do with money, and therefore the market cannot profit from them. Your right to enjoy them comes by birth and subsequent good conduct (that is, by God's will and personal virtue). To make people into "labor" and "consumers" meant depriving them of these unbought advantages.

It also meant depriving them of an orderly and fruitful environmentalism (Polanyi, writing in 1944, made too little of this). It meant taking away the subsistence base people held in common—fields (in the early days), forests, rivers and ocean. Such things, cultivated or harvested according to local custom and laws, gave people a subsistence that depended only locally on market conditions. This subsistence base was an obstacle, therefore, to the coming of a nationally organized industry and economy. Bruce Brown suggests, for instance, that the destruction of fish in English rivers was a *precondition* of industrialization: now the countryside could not support the people. They would no longer be its neighbors. The earth was to be reserved for industrial uses.

The industrial culture was created, then, by a war on people that was also, inevitably, a war on the earth. Polanyi is eloquently adequate about the war on people. Legislation "emancipat[ed] the laborer" from the traditional community, he wrote, "for the avowed purpose of making the threat of . . . hunger effective"—or roughly the same tactics Stalin used to collectivize Soviet farming, with similarly horrifying callousness about human life. The difference is that Stalin was using exceptional means for a specific ideological end; whereas the hostility of industry to traditional communities is part of our normal life. An industrial economy detaches people from the earth for two reasons: to make us depend for subsistence on the market; and to gain access to the earth we would, in self-defense, protect.

The Earth-Careful Community
It is easy to praise "community" in the abstract, without having much sense of what we mean. It is easy to sentimentalize traditional societies. (Anthropologists have often written in an elegiac vein, anthropology being an invention of the society that is destroying the traditional society under study. In this sense, native people were right about cameras: they do kill, or at least embalm.)

For much of American society, the ideal of "community" is a secular version of the body of believers—a dream of a secure emotional context with no requirements as to belief. But community in the abstract is not a Band-Aid or a universal pill or a form of providence. It will not, by itself, solve the dilemmas and heal the self-woundings of human life.

Putting the question of community in ecological terms, however, sharpens it considerably. It becomes (something like) the question, How is it practical for us to live? when "practical" means "sustainable in the given natural conditions of the planet." The answer is (something like), It is practical for us to live in small coherent communities, and not otherwise.

Here we run into a problem of definition. What size is "small"? How large can a community become without losing its coherence? A village can feel whole, integral—but what about a small city? A single church, potentially—but what about a denomination?

We cannot solve the problem with numbers, however, because it is not a numerical problem. The solution is moral and psychological, and is suggested by Marty Strange in his defense of family farms when he asks, "How big is the typical farm in the family farm system?" and answers, "It is about as big as its neighbors." That is, a community extends as far as you can have neighbors—as far as you can have personal knowledge of, and take effective personal responsibility for, other people and places other than your own. The student who bicycled down my country road had no neighborhood with anything there. The community of Dorothy Wordsworth's journal entry was so powerful that it made the earth, in specific fields and pastures, into a neighbor.

But Strange's example says more than that, because it raises the question of subsistence, of necessity. This is the question we began with by beginning in the supermarket: How are we to conduct the commerce with nature necessary to feed ourselves? Our answer so far in the industrial era has been that a global marshaling of scientific knowledge, money and fossil fuel will force the earth to support us. This will seem true, however, only if we accept a further assumption: that most of us should be "freed" (as we say) from having to participate in providing our own subsistence. Only when we get out of the way can the machine, and the multinational, have their opportunity.

The premise of an earth-careful culture, by contrast, is that as many people as possible should have responsibility for looking after the earth. They should have the chance, that is, to learn the knowledge and virtues that are required. They cannot do this, however, without the help, the common wisdom and the mutual accountability of a genuine community. These are the resources and restraints that make looking after the earth possible.

This connection between communities and subsistence is one of the most important things Wendell Berry has taught us. If we need healthy land in order to eat, agricultural land also needs the direct care of responsible people; the obligation is, so to speak, reciprocal, between fertile soil and a community stable and wise to care for it.

To what degree community itself implies, or supplies, the necessary virtues is a complicated question. Alasdair MacIntyre has argued that any human project demands virtue just to function: there would have to be honor among thieves, or nothing would get stolen. Historically, however, communities often do wrong; and what is more, they derive some of their cohesiveness from doing it. Bullies and militarist nations get along fine as long as they have someone to bully.

The distinction here is between virtues internal to the community—the ones that hold it together—and its external vices. The environmental crisis transcends the distinction: it has made us realize, as we often say, that all humanity and the whole planet are joined in one enterprise, from which nothing is "external." All our virtues and vices will eventually come home to us in good and bad effects.

Another way of saying this is that necessity brings morality out of hiding. We are living, as Schumacher said, in the convergence of wisdom and practical sanity. The practical effects of virtue and vice are clear now for anyone who wants to look.

But this is not enough by itself. For us to exercise practical goodness, it must have direct, personal substance for us. Community, that is, is the link between necessity and morality, or between survival and goodness. The known circle of people and places turns goodness into actable obligation. Goodness is something you owe your neighbors, something you will feel the result of doing. The obligation to a rainforest is too distant and abstract. It takes all of the power of the media to keep it in our minds. But the field next door faces you every time you look out the window.

Action and Paralysis

Americans live in a paradox with regard to morality. Right to life and right to choose, minority causes, governmental and corporate immorality, not to speak of the cheaper immoralities of the tabloid and the soap opera, keep us in a perpetual discontent. Still our paralysis in the face of moral issues is a commonplace. We are constantly troubled and seldom effective.

It is also obvious that we do change things, decisively, when we find ourselves acting in defense of our homes and our children. What we call our "values" come into play when we are fighting for valued *people* and valued *places*. We are paralyzed before the deterioration of the earth because we mostly lack a local "real world," a community, to defend.

This is the lesson of grassroots environmental protest: the Love Canal protest against toxic waste, the similar movement against pollution in the Louisiana "chemical corridor" and the opposition to nuclear waste dumping in rural western New York recounted in John Leax's *Standing Ground* (1991).

But communities would not be emergency things in an established earth-careful way of life. They would be the norm. And the virtues of community would be, or could be, general. Virtues are not like technical knowledge, the concern of one profession or form of education. If they are not attempted by everyone in a community, they have no authority over anyone. If teachers and salespeople are not responsible for the earth in their places, it is unjust, and unrealistic, to expect farmers and Forest Service supervisors to be responsible in theirs. For the effectual care of the earth, you must have communities in place whose whole way of life is frugal, peaceable, temperate and constant.

Keeping to Ourselves

It is as obvious as our moral disquiet that we Americans live comparatively restless, isolated and anonymous lives. It is potentially an error, though, to think that our failures at community are failures pure and simple—that we have been trying all along to preserve community and have only not managed. We must keep Polanyi's thesis in mind: industrial society had to destroy communities. They are its natural enemy, because they preserve and nourish things it needs to exploit. They offer free, in return for membership, what the market needs to sell for profit.

Modern thinking about society repeats one distinction obsessively—the distinction (in Ferdinand Tönnies's famous terms) between *gemeinschaft* (or traditional community) and *gesellschaft* (modern "rational" society). Writing in the 1880s, Tönnies saw the move from one to the other as society's growing up; modern society was adult. *Gemeinschaften* were responses to physical necessity. They had to be orderly, stable and conscientious to survive. The *gesellschaft* freed us from necessity—from necessary labor, that is, and therefore (so the argument went) from superstition and social restrictions.

This freedom was the gift of modern technology—a freedom from labor and from scarcity at the same time. Machines would channel nature toward producing a flood of useful things. Free of necessity, people would make communities voluntarily, not because they had to. Communities could be like the intellectual, aesthetic and patriotic brotherhoods, clubs and circles that the German bourgeois of Tönnies's day joined to uplift the spirit and improve the mind.

We fiddle obsessively with this distinction because, as Christopher Lasch observes, we cannot escape the fear that the difference between kinds of society is an ethical difference as well—that in swapping the moral and practical clarity of the village for the freedom of the modern city, we have lost a necessary frame for understanding and disciplining social life as a whole.

For in twentieth-century America we have taken the notion of voluntary community a step further: it is essential to our idea of freedom that *individuals* set the terms for *communities*, and not the other way around. We hold communities together; they cannot hold us together. We don't belong to a church, really; we join it temporarily, on sufferance. Now churches must sell themselves to the shopper—they advertise, week by week, in the newspaper, sometimes even on the entertainment page—and the shopper may join and drop half a dozen churches, one after another, depending on whether they suit. Whatever this open market in faiths means for spreading the gospel, it is clear what it means for practicing it: how are we to learn the ways of this spiritual neighborhood? We never know who our neighbors are.

When we think about the loss of community, then, we should remember that it is a premise of modern culture that we do not *have* to have communities at all. The modern city, which offers so many random experiences, so many provisional selves, has been raised in the absence of community. What Emile Durkheim, Tönnies's great successor, formulated as an explanation for urban suicide—*anomie,* the loss of a significant context—is actually the city's promise: that people can live there without obligation, friendship, commitment, dependence or self-restraint, and still expect the market to work to support them.

This discovery is one of the insights of novels in the industrial age. "He had got completely away from everyone, like a tortoise in its shell," Dostoevsky says about Raskolnikov, the murderer in *Crime and Punishment.* Not everyone who lives in a city lives, or wants to live, such a life; but this life is in the logic of the city, where the market concentrates its productivity, where anything can be had for money.

In this the city merely extends the logic of modern culture. Freedom from necessity finally removes nature from contact with other parts of life. It creates the climate of sheer fact—"Facts alone are wanted in life," says Dickens's Gradgrind, another character from a city novel. It also drains our moral and spiritual lives of substance, by taking away the practical need to exercise virtues. These virtues are not needed after all; all that we need is money, or a place in the market where money may be made. We do not have to be good to be comfortable, or even to survive.

Tönnies, Durkheim and Dickens did not live long enough to see the result of this. But it is plain to us: its name is the exhaustion of the earth, by a market without moral restraints. Necessity, it turns out, was not overcome, only postponed: the surplus of goods and services is only possible for a limited time, for a few people. Community, apparently, is not voluntary; if we do not learn to live with neighbors, we may not live. Apparently we will have to live under obligation, with charity, after all.

The Mosquito Trap

It is a kind of oblique evidence for this fact that even the consumer market, in whose name traditional communities are destroyed, must appeal to our hunger for community to keep us buying. The distributor's truck at the supermarket dock is wearing a slogan like "Serving the American Coffee Drinker Since 1955." Now serving, genuine servanthood, is possible only among neighbors. It defines the motive for sharing labor without demanding payment. But the truck only pulls up to the dock because money draws it.

The slogan uses, and cheapens, a crucial practical and scriptural principle that is also a principle of workable community. The market also preys on and cheapens the ordinary small everyday bonds that tie people together. In a store the other day I discovered an "Official Michigan Mosquito Trap," made in China, stuck to a card where "Michigan" had been inserted in a space left blank for any state or place name.

To be caught by the trap a mosquito would have to be as big as a sparkplug, which was of course the joke. The ferocity of local insects is the kind of joke that ties a community to its natural place. But there was nothing spontaneous, local or funny about the bit of market junk I saw; it was just a consumer item.

What the market offers in place of communal ties to a local place is a "lifestyle," the predesigned mode of consuming that mimics a way of life. You can have a Ralph Lauren "Western" room—"Indian" rug (no Native Americans have touched it), a "Mexican" chair (ditto), a "pioneer" fireplace (there are no more pioneers)—in your Cape Cod in Georgia, none of it implying the slightest connection with an actual community in place or with the historical experience of any.

Yet the dependence of the consumer market on community is deeper even than these thefts and parodies. The corporation that supplies the market will practice the virtues of community within itself, because without them (as MacIntyre would say) no organized effort at anything is possible. The corporation will be a community—an authoritarian one, probably, with a clear end in view and using the threat of unemployment to enforce loyalty. That is, the institution that sells the freedom to try anything cannot afford to operate in these terms. No real community can. Even a commitment to pay dividends—morally speaking, a minimal commitment—requires a focus and a sacrifice of individual autonomy no church in our society can expect.

The Burden of Belonging

Just across the river from where I sit is an abandoned gravel quarry, fenced and posted with "Keep Out" signs. It is growing up in poplars and bushes, but it is an ugly place, where the ground was gouged, ransacked and then abandoned. The warnings are purely legal. The people who live around the pit will never be a concern to the corporation unless a child scrambles into a hole and is hurt.

The land was used and then left. It is no one's neighbor, nor is it (except for birds and the trade in ragweed seed) a neighbor of the land around it. The corporation maintains a handsome office building in Grand Rapids—I have driven past it—but it is no one's neighbor: the distance between where it does business and the land that business has affected is the same as the distance between the corporation's people and the people who live by the pit. It is our small stripmine, without the acid seepage and mudslides, but with the same scrupulously legal harm to the place and neglect of the local community.

The argument of this chapter comes to this: our natural environment cannot be cared for but through extensive, direct, personal responsibility for it; and this responsibility is only practical, finally, in self-conscious communities. We need an ethics, a theology and a politics that will feed the life of such communities.

It is customary at this point to make reservations about such an argument. We feel compelled to say what we do *not* mean: we don't mean that everyone should be a farmer; we don't mean that everyone must live in the country.

I do not, as a matter of fact, mean these things; but (as Thoreau said) I mean something more like them than we may be comfortable with. The trouble with reservations is that they turn into excuses: if we don't have to live in the country (we think) then we don't have to make ways to take extensive, direct, personal responsibility for the condition of the earth in our places. We can leave all of that to someone who likes it. But the fact is that, farmer or not, city-dweller or not, this is precisely what we have to do.

There is a spiritual principle here. "Carry one another's burdens," Paul says in Galatians. A moment later he speaks of the "family of faith." This law that makes family is the practical articulation of the commandment to love your neighbor.

Now you cannot love your neighbor by starving her children or poisoning the earth they play on. We cannot take up one another's human burdens, then, without taking up the burden of the earth, which is our common inheritance and home, and whose health or illness penetrates everything that we do. We live in a culture that breaks families of all kinds, and leaves increasing amounts of land to be consumed by a few on our general behalf. Such places have no neighbors, human or natural. No communities, large or small, exist to serve them and bind them to other places. And yet to be a neighbor to such a place is to accomplish two desirable things at once: to nurture and protect the place; and to discover that you belong there.

6
THREE
HISTORICAL
EXAMPLES

I KNOW SEVERAL HUMANITARIANS AND
THEY ARE ALL FEROCIOUS.

GEORGE BERNARD SHAW

O*ne way of thinking about the environmental crisis is to see it as* a series of specific and shocking emergencies—the emergency of landfill space; the emergency of atmospheric warming; the emergency of arable land erosion; oil spills; species extinction; famine.

The intention of this book is to remind us that all of these emergencies have common ground—that we decimate species by spilling the oil with which our cars heat the atmosphere; that the landfills are full of the convenience packaging that carried food raised on marginal land at the cost of someone else's subsistence. It is our common way of life—it makes no practical difference how ignorantly we carry it on—that is doing the damage.

The social facts of our life—the worship of excess, the backdropping of nature and people, the loss of community—are all causes of our danger. And all of them have histories longer than the environmental crisis; it is the latest fruit of older evils. The older they are, the more natural they seem to us—and the harder for us to grasp them or to conceive of a change.

Therefore we need to remind ourselves that cultural events are not fated. They happen by choice, and by choices; and sometimes the particular choices occur often enough, consistently enough, that we can say that the larger event these choices pointed to happened because we wanted it to happen.

The three historical examples in this chapter illustrate one such larger event. (They are not histories, even partial, of the events they refer to.) These examples connect the coming of the industrial and technological culture with the backdropping of people. They illustrate the breaking of communal subsistence that Polanyi saw as necessary to modern society—the enforced separation of people from the earth, their expropriation, their unsettlement; the basic condition, that is, for a way of life that destroys the earth.

The Giant of Giant Castle

England was the first nation to contain, or create, a modern industrial society. The breaking of communal subsistence there went on for a long time, with many ends in view, and an industrial society coming into view only at the close—so that the four-century process (roughly 1450-1850) finally resembles a long marathon in which, unexpectedly, with a massive shot of adrenaline, the last lap was the fastest.

In England the breaking of communal subsistence was known as "enclosure"—the process by which fields, meadows and forest margin held in common by the inhabitants of a village were fenced in for private use. The land thus taken away from its workers could be agriculturally "improved"—it could be made more profitable to farm—but the extra food, and the profits, went to the landowner who put up the capital for improvements. Enclosure therefore meant uprooting the traditional communities on the land; it sometimes meant introducing farming methods that injured the land; and it meant the enrichment of those with the political power to force enclosure—first monasteries, then merchants and aristocratic landowners, and finally the mill owners bent on modernizing England's economy. Enclosure's profits provided the capital for the Industrial Revolution.

Enclosure had two striking demographic results: it emptied agricultural land of its people, and it swelled the mass of the more or less permanently homeless. Of the two, depopulation struck contemporary observers most sharply. Thomas More wrote in 1516 that enclosing abbots "throw down houses: they pluck down towns, and leave nothing standing, but only the church to be made a sheephouse." Oliver Goldsmith's well-known lament *The Deserted Village* (1770) puts obvious, primary emphasis on desertion: the country village had been evacuated. Its kind of civil life had been destroyed. Somewhat later a successful encloser was recorded (by Marx) to have said: "I look around, and not a house is to be seen but mine. I am the giant of Giant Castle, and have eaten up all my neighbours." This did not, of course, keep him from investing his profits.

The emptiness of the countryside, the absence of houses, chimney smoke and human voices in the fields, struck observers so sharply because they were assuming—remembering, really—the ancient georgic ideal of arable land occupied by settled communities. In these communities, for centuries, people had married, reared children and worked the fields, almost, as Peter Laslett says, in one action. The communities were also religious. They husbanded their faith and sacramental life; the church had been the center of the village, the meeting place. More's fury at the church degraded into a "sheephouse" was a reaction to the change in the focus of rural life from traditional faith to new money.

Enclosure has been the subject of a good deal of controversy. It has been interpreted as an example of class war—though well-off peasants often joined in the enclosure "by agreement," to make themselves better off—and as one cause of the English agricultural revolution. But enclosure was as much ecological as political or economic. It broke the link between land and communities to care for it. Enclosure initiated the modern treatment of the earth, as an exploitable backdrop to cultural life.

England in 1800 saw the same paradox as Third World nations see today: more food is grown but more people starve. The principle behind the paradox is the same: "enclosure by men with capital" (as Christopher Hill puts it), "brutally disregarding the rights of commoners," will produce food; but it destroys livelihoods. The food goes where money draws it, not to those who raise it. The secure pattern of subsistence is broken. What breaks with it is the intimate local care of the land.

Not that communal farming before enclosure had been ideal: medieval manor accounts are speckled with notes about *terra debilis,* worn-out land. But the commoners came up with their own alternatives to enclosure—for instance, the religious and agronomic vision of the seventeenth-century "Digger," Gerard Winstanley. (The "Diggers" got their name by occupying land and digging it as a protest against enclosure.) "True religion and undefiled," Winstanley wrote, "is to let every one quietly have earth to manure"—earth, that is, to grow crops that will winter the herds whose manure fertilizes the fields. It is the classic cycle of traditional agriculture, as old as Virgil's *Georgics* and as new as "third-wave" alternative farms. It would have repaired *terra debilis;* it is what the Amish do.

Captain Swing

Enclosure's second demographic effect was the increase of "masterless men"—homelessness. For two centuries the Elizabethan Poor Law (1601) tried to put the homeless to work, as the Act of Settlement (1662) tried to get them to stay put and be looked after. Enclosure never favored such measures. As its profits began to feed industrial expansion, industry demanded workers, labor, "hands"; they came, inevitably, from among the homeless who, as long as they were *not* settled, would go (as Adam

Smith argued) where the market wanted them.

The Industrial Revolution, predictably, speeded enclosures. (It was the adrenaline that turned the last lap into a sprint.) The trickle of parliamentary enclosing acts became, after 1760, a storm—in a few decades, 5,400 separate enclosures in 4,200 acts swept up seven million acres, or about 20 percent of England's land area. People driven off their land were driven by hunger into the cities, where the looms of the cotton mills awaited them. The modern urban mass population was created, with its two interlocking functions—to provide industrial labor and to consume industrial products.

The horrors of this creation are familiar: they were recorded early on by Friedrich Engels, walking in his well-bred shoes through the tenements and courtyards full of standing excrement "below Ducie Bridge" in Manchester in 1844. It is not surprising that this violence on human life was met by violence. In the early 1800s, the Luddites smashed industrial looms in the cities while gangs who called themselves "Captain Swing" smashed primitive threshing machines in the countryside. The gangs did not, of course, grasp the new financial and social structure that was providing the thought and money for the new England. Burning a hayrick or breaking a loom did nothing to stop such profound change.

In another sense, however, it was an appropriate and even measured response. (A farmer customarily received a note of warning and explanation before his machines were smashed.) Captain Swing saw, correctly, that what was under attack was a whole way of life. To move from handwork and homework to machine and factory was to change everything about the culture. It crossed the distance between tools, which extend a human's capacity to be human, and machines, which replace the human altogether.

The question for Captain Swing was what place a human would have in his or her culture. The prevailing answer was that it would be a place defined by money. Everything, finally, would be sacrificed to this—family, community, skill and personal accomplishment, the link between the person and the earth that guaranteed subsistence.

An Insatiable Desire After Land

Since we have observed the five-hundredth anniversary of Columbus's landing, it is worth reflecting that we began our European history on this continent with the conquistadores' ideal of vast wealth acquired by conquest, not with the opposite ideal of sufficiency gained by faithfulness. We have been conquering things ever since: the Native American, the continent's sheer size, its wild natural abundance. Every conquest has brought us profits, and every one has made us poorer.

Enclosure came much later to rural America than to rural England, and it came under different names and in new forms. Most of America, unlike most of England, had no established landowning class to control and profit from enclosure, and to use its profits to strengthen its own continuing authority. For the first three centuries of our agrarian history, moreover, the frontier made possession of land the result of a free-for-all. Out of this grew a different ideology, not less destructive—not control of land to enforce an established hierarchy, but acquisition of land to force-feed economic expansion.

England had a severely limited land base; it was the cheap availability of land in America that broke the first, archetypal American communities. Early New England towns were more stable and independent even than their European pattern: independent out of necessity (they had no surrounding economic and technological infrastructure to depend on); stable by design. They had been designed as "cities on a hill"—living demonstrations of how the gospel in its English and low-country Puritan form was to be lived.

Thus the circle of heavily built, inner-directed houses around a "common" that was usually mud and rough pasturage, but headed by a meeting-house: the circle was refuge, focus, social scaffold, camp of the new Israel. Outside it lay the common fields. Outside them, the forest, invaded shallowly for fuel and timber, but mostly impenetrable, the wilderness, the antithesis of civil life.

The village's physical shape signified a common life. The earliest Puritan colonists were not individualists in search of fortunes: "though thou hast two thousands to spend," wrote grim John Cotton, "yet if thou hast no calling, tending to publique good, thou art an uncleane beast."

It did not last long. By 1654, or the end of the first generation, most of the designed villages had frayed away into scattered settlements. The bait was partly land—"There hath been in many [church members] an insatiable desire after land," said the Synod of 1679—and agricultural profits. But the temptation was also, as Charles Chauncy noted in 1655, that people in the woods were free of the communal pattern of living— free of the restraints of a conscience answerable to "common good." They were free to hack down the forests and burn them and plough among the stumps, and move on when the thin soil was spent.

They had become, that is, pioneers. They had no time or (as they saw it) need for earth-care. By 1700, "making" farmland, they had cut so much woodland that parts of New England faced a timber shortage. De Tocqueville commented that Americans never noticed forests until they were falling. The first laws protecting wildlife—the first mark, that is, of waste and extremity—were passed in New York in 1708.

Economic Development

There is no room here for a history of American expansion: only for a contrast of stories about it. The familiar story—initiated, perhaps, by Frederick Jackson Turner's well-known 1893 essay on the frontier—tells how the frontier virtues, self-reliance and practical resourcefulness, built institutions that transcended the frontier. Rural economies were succeeded by manifest destiny and industrialization. Jefferson's vision of a commonwealth of agrarian communities led, finally, to something altogether different. The other story is more complex. It adds three considerations.

First, frontier history is not a story of the transcendence of one way of life by another—not the healthy evolution of something better—but a story of destruction. Or, more precisely, a story of a parasite feeding on the body of its host.

The process was in many ways another case of enclosure. Beginning especially in the 1880s, urban investment in farming—in cash crops such as cotton, tobacco, grain and cattle—had two complementary results: it increased agricultural production and profits; and it decreased the need for farmers. The profits went directly into industrial expansion. The farmers were displaced to the cities to provide labor and an urban market. That is, the farmer paid to reduce himself to dependence on an economy alien both from the land and from the rural community.

The second consideration is that this enclosure was not, as in England, gradual and improvisatory, but has been to a large extent deliberate. We do not have to resort to a conspiracy theory to face the fact that neither American economics, education nor government has had any real investment in preserving rural communities.

"The countryside found a place fashioned for it within the urban system," Alan Trachtenberg writes of the 1880s: "it became an impoverished zone, a market colony, a cheap source of food, labor, and certain raw materials." The theory behind this process has been stated and defended explicitly by economists such as Jane Jacobs. That the countryside is despoiled in the process—that the process only works as long as the countryside exists to be despoiled—does not occur as an objection. And the only counsel for country people is that they leave for the cities as soon as possible.

Which is what government and education have been preaching for decades. The Committee on Economic Development, organized during World War II, took as its goal the reduction of rural population as a way of increasing the return on agricultural investments, swelling the urban work force and driving food prices down. Much of its program was realized by government policy—by the shift to flexible price supports in 1954, for instance, which was used to put small farmers out of business;

or by the support of large exporting agriculture in the late 1970s, which had the result, when foreign markets faltered, of bankrupting family farms by the thousands. The trend, of course, continues.

Aftershock

The third consideration is to see that the story of rural colonization is a story of environmental damage as well. An industrial economy that feeds on rural capital is feeding on land. That is, after all, where a farm economy gets its capital: it raises crops that turn fertility into a marketable commodity. The question is whether this process will further the farmer's welfare, and ultimately the land's, or will maximize the market's profits. In an industrial economy such as we have had since the 1880s, the answer is a foregone conclusion.

How the shrinking of farm communities produces the harm our arable land is suffering is the theme of Wendell Berry's classic *The Unsettling of America* (1977) and of more recent studies such as Marty Strange's *Family Farming* (1988). Industrial agriculture implies large farms devoted to a single crop, large machinery and large-scale consumption of chemicals: it implies, that is, few people, fewer eyes to watch the field, fewer hands to care for it.

It is true that the same decades that incorporated America (to use Trachtenberg's phrase), in part at the expense of traditional agriculture, also saw the birth of the environmental movement—the first national parks, the first public fights in defense of wilderness, the first of what we might call "environmental tourism." Like the early game-protection laws, these were marks of extremity. They came as an aftershock of damage. They revealed an implicit awareness that if something was not done, everything might be lost—that the juggernaut of national "prosperity," within a few years of its first machine, was threatening to consume everything in sight.

And yet, according to Aldo Leopold's principle—too much cherishing of wilderness destroys it—the compensatory defense of wilderness did not go to the heart of the matter. Our crucial obligation had been, and is now, to design a cultural life that would respect nature both inhabited and uninhabited. But we Americans have failed at that from the start.

Killing Africa

But of course the clearest examples of traditional cultures starving on misused land are not now in the industrial world. Here the great transformation was completed some time ago, and we have borne the costs—or rather some of us, immigrants, slaves, migrant labor, rural populations, people with few audible voices, have borne terrible costs most of the rest of us have forgotten. Today's agony is greater and more visible: the broken communities lie on three continents.

"Africa is dying," Lloyd Timberlake wrote five years ago, "because in its ill-planned ill-advised attempt to 'modernise' itself it has cut itself in pieces." What we see as a problem with African *nature,* such as drought-induced famine, is frequently a case of people deprived of traditional subsistence—people vulnerable to, deprived of their long familiar defenses against, natural stresses. The planning of this has often been African; the advice, mostly Western and international.

It is too easy to blame international projects for the failures of small nations. As Conor Cruise O'Brien remarked some time ago, the developed nations' impulse to blame themselves for all of the Third World's problems is just the flip side of imperialism: the belief, in both cases, that the only true dynamic in human affairs is modern, Western and technological.

Which is clearly not the case: there would be no point in regretting the death of traditional cultures if it were. Still, peasant cultures have sustained enormous pressure even from the West's best-publicized efforts to help them: for instance, the "Green Revolution." Begun in Mexico in the forties as an effort to breed crop varieties specifically suited to Third World conditions, the revolution came quickly to have two broader goals: to alleviate world hunger and to help small nations obtain foreign-exchange capital for economic growth. More food was supposed to feed more people at home and provide an exportable surplus.

How the peasant's grain was to compete with the subsidized surpluses of America and Europe will be worth considering in a moment. Apart from one or two instances, in any case, the revolution has failed its promise: "hunger, malnutrition, rural unemployment, and rural violence have remained intractable," writes one observer. "There is no evidence," say two others, "to suppose that . . . a high-technology, export-oriented agriculture has in any way alleviated the food deficiencies of the peoples of Latin America."

What needs explaining, clearly, is why, with genuine compassion and international political will and scientific savvy, the revolution has so often been a violent failure. With all due room for qualifications, the main reason is plain: the revolution is our form of the breaking of communal subsistence.

Tomatoes from Mexico

What the revolution offers, essentially, is American industrial agriculture: a "package" (as it is called) containing HYVs (high-yield varieties), agricultural chemicals, irrigation plans, complex schedules for farmwork and modern marketing. Even if we put the revolution's aims modestly, its plan obviously implies much of what we identify with the life of advanced societies: the HYVs created by sophisticated biological science, the chemicals produced by multinationals, the marketing provided by international business.

To the revolution, then, as Andrew Pearse says in a United Nations-sponsored study, the traditional culture always seems backward and obstructive. Its destruction is seen as both desirable and inevitable: "from the logic of the process," wrote Robert Heilbroner in one of the testaments of progress, "there is no escape." "The very fabric of traditional societies," a report told an American president, "must be rewoven."

The trouble with that sentence is that revolutions do not reweave things; they tear things apart and replace them. The Green Revolution—like the *conquest* of hunger and the *war* on poverty—has violence in its name and conception: violence that, if the thrust of social effort gets distracted even slightly, falls on the people and the earth.

For the Third World nation must pay for its "package" of seeds and chemicals. It pays first by selling forests, mineral resources and fishing rights. It may have a saleable surplus of rice or wheat. But the international market generally does not need the surplus of subsistence foods that the peasants grow to feed themselves. The market wants coffee, sugar, luxury fruits, seasonal vegetables out of season; and the nation adjusts by devoting its best land to monoculture—in Sudan, this meant sugar and cotton plantations along the Nile—and pushing native communities onto marginal land. Even farms in Mexico initially devoted to irrigated HYVs have turned into privately owned farms for the American luxury market, while Mexico buys American grain by exporting oil.

The cumulative effects of paying for the package are ecological disaster: the deforestation of watersheds, like that which produced the destructive Philippine floods of late 1991; desertification, as has resulted from the dispossession of traditional farming and nomadic peoples by industrial farming in East Africa; erosion; famine and disease. Again, the tie that was broken to accomplish all of this is the tie between traditional communities with long experience in subsistence farming, grazing and gathering, and their ancestral land. It is the unsettling, now, of Latin America, Asia and Africa.

The predictable response to such criticism of the Green Revolution is that, given the increase of Third World population, something has to be done. This is true; but it is not a defense of what we have done. We have come, very late, to see the rationality of working with traditional subsistence communities instead of against them.

The lesson is not that peasant societies should be preserved out of anthropological or poetic interest. (Certainly not that they should be preserved as tourist attractions.) The lesson is just the opposite: they must be preserved, or actually restored, *on practical grounds*. These grounds include what we would call environmental concerns: the ecological balance and modesty of long-standing traditional agriculture are an invaluable practical wisdom. The question is whether we in the First World are willing to learn from those in the Third whom we have offered to instruct.

Disciplining Change

The first clear victory of industrial society over traditional community can be dated with some precision. Karl Polanyi's date is 1834. In that year the Poor Law Amendment Act (or "New Poor Law") abolished the last social recourse of the English poor; no parish or paternal landowner would help them now; they would work, for inadequate wages, in the factories, or they would starve.

Even that, however, was only a beginning, or perhaps the end of the beginning. Traditional societies still occupied most of the globe, and the coming of industrial society has been, since then, the history of strain between new and old. And there have always been communities, almost always religious, that have defied industrial society and preserved their own communal lives inside it. North of where I sit to write this, Amish farmers are buying land ruined by industrial potato-farming, and bringing it back, as they do, to fertility. Since we are still, officially, committed to breaking traditional communities, it is worth pausing for a moment to think about one that has refused to be broken.

The Amish are a hopeful example precisely because they have survived for so long, intact, in the center of industrial society. They have had time, as well as the resources, wisdom and patience, to fight the complicated legal and economic battles that this survival has required. They understood, for instance, that they would not survive without the right to teach their own children. Amish schoolhouses were necessary to Amish fields. Ecological sanity depends on a way of life, kept intact in community; and this vital keeping is the business of education.

The Amish depend on the biblical principle of the "body of believers." In this sense, no one is born Amish. You become Amish by committing yourself to the local body. This commitment has given the Amish the power to change and adapt. Different bodies of Amish have different *ordnungen*, or community rules, and these shape different customs—some use only horses, some use other kinds of traction power in addition. Where our desperate, irrational scarcity of farmland keeps these wonderful farmers off the land, they can and will do other work.

One of a community's powers, then, is the power to change intelligently. No one will deny that traditional societies, say, in the Third World, could benefit from improvements in medical care, sanitation, appropriate technologies. An argument against destructive change is not an argument for stasis.

But the project of improvement always raises two questions: Who will dictate the form of these improvements? and, How fast will the culture be required to change?

The notion of a cultural tradition, as Alasdair MacIntyre has shown, does not preclude change. Social forms can change around the tradition, just as the tradition itself can entertain debate and development and remain a tradition. Anthropologists sent out by government agencies, moreover, repeatedly come back with the report that traditional communities can accept rational change. The peasant cultivator, after all, knows his inherited land better than anyone else in the world—certainly better than the Green Revolution expert flown in for a two-week visit. The peasant knows how the land has tolerated what he and his father and grandfather have done.

The peasant community's tradition, further, is moral and makes moral requirements: the peasant can recognize just and unjust dealing. Latin American peasantries have been waiting for political and economic justice for generations.

We do not have to impose change, then, for change to come. As for the speed of change, E. F. Schumacher put it very clearly:

If the nature of change is such that nothing is left for fathers to teach their sons and mothers their daughters, or for the sons to accept from their fathers, family life collapses. . . . Social cohesion, cooperation, mutual respect, and above all, self-respect, courage in the face of adversity, and the ability to bear hardships—all this and much else disintegrates.

There is an observable, experiential limit to the pace of change; and the limit has something to do with the virtues that hold a community together.

Limiting the speed of change does not mean refusing to change at all. It means preserving the moral securities that make change tolerable. But these securities are of no value in an industrial society. It specializes in rapid and destructive change—in change, that is, that no one *can* adapt to except on the market's terms. This is what smashes intact communities into undifferentiated labor and mass consumers. This is what takes traditional communities off their land and allows "rational"—that is, industrial—uses to monopolize it.

Fast Food

From its start in fifteenth-century England, the breaking of communal subsistence went on, in large part, because it enriched a powerful social minority. At first there was comparatively little pressure to justify the fact that many were suffering to enrich a few: these few were the ones whom God evidently favored, the born aristocrats. In the nineteenth century, when the sufferings grew worldwide and the people who profited were no longer generally aristocrats, another rationale was required. It took the form of the Caiaphas argument: many were suffering for a greater good—namely, the coming of the technological culture. No matter if (generally speaking) the many were not given a choice about their suffering; or if (generally speaking) they were sacrificed for a future they could not enjoy themselves.

The argument would sound better if, with the profits, we had in fact built a just and equitable society—one that disciplines technology within moral restraints and compensates everyone's work. It is obvious that we have done no such thing. We have not built a society that would use the resources of the planet for the good of all her children, or even most. The breaking of communal subsistence continues, and it continues to enrich minorities. It may not be too much of an exaggeration to say that what we have built in place of a sustainable society is the fast-food restaurant.

Even more than the supermarket, the fast-food place is an icon of the environmental crisis. Here you meet the reduction of subsistence to a technological problem—the standardized sandwich brought by warehouse and truck from an international system of production—and the backdropping of earth and people.

In one of these restaurants, now, you can find a brochure promising that the beef served there was not grazed on rainforest land. Whatever this means in the technicalities of the law—does land that was rainforest five years ago qualify?—the brochure makes a necessary connection for us: it connects what the technological culture has made of food with the death of subsistence communities. The fast-food sandwich is what some of us have gained for the suffering of many others. It is what we have gained for the wreckage of the earth.

7
The
CHEAP-
ENERGY
GOSPEL

THE TEMPLE IS HOLY
BECAUSE IT IS NOT FOR SALE.

EZRA POUND

I *went into the convenience store—not a 7-Eleven, but a cramped* little grocery remodeled for the trade in beer and snack food, the floor still wooden, the glass-doored coolers stacked with cans and ending a foot below the old stamped-tin ceiling. I asked the proprietor for a postcard. The man beside me looked up, dragging his six-pack off the counter, and said, "Of Rapid City?" He laughed, turning to walk out the door.

I was in Rapid City because my mother had been born there seventy years before, when the town had a mill employing a hundred workers, a train depot and two hotels, while the timber in the Michigan woods that engulfed the town was being cut and shipped south to the furniture factories in Grand Rapids. As long as the timber held out, the town was alive and important to itself. Then the woods had all left on the railroad.

The line shriveled back to Traverse City, the mill closed, the hotels shut down, people left. It was the time of the death of small towns.

Lumbering was an extractive industry, like coal mining and oil drilling, and played out in a few decades. (What we have done in the Third World we practiced first on ourselves.) The death of small towns is connected not just with the growth of the economy but with a certain attitude toward land—that it is a resource to be exploited, not a home to be known, cherished and made fruitful.

Rapid City is not a ghost town; it is one of thousands of small American towns that seem to survive without visible means of support. Such towns are another form of broken community. They are fragments reputedly swept up in the global village, but actually isolated, left behind, in doubt. Rapid City accepts the American orthodoxy that its only felicity lies in duplicating the urban economy. By this standard it is of course a failure, and so it sees itself; and the hype, therefore, that it hopes will draw tourists to its surrounding woods begins and ends in shame.

This is why the guy beside me, with his six-pack and his Caterpillar hat, dumped his embittered laugh—"Of Rapid City?"—in front of me on the counter, like change.

Travail

A hundred years ago there was an exodus of German farmers from Pennsylvania and Ontario into Michigan, and with them Mennonite preachers. Among the first to come was my great-grandfather, Elder Bernhard Kreutziger. According to the official history of his church, he came in 1884 to build a congregation in Brown City, where a large Mennonite camp meeting would in time grow up.

A few years later his son, my grandfather, came to live in Rapid City and to pastor two or three small congregations, driving a horse and buggy through the countryside on a regular circuit. In the winter, he drove a sleigh. Sometimes he was paid in money; sometimes with a chicken and feed for his horse. Like so many men in his generation and before—but not since—Simon Kreutziger was a fine natural carpenter. As he preached, he built churches for his people to meet in.

He had a powerful Mennonite sense of the church as a body—not the church universal, but the circle of people, however small, that belonged to one place and one mutual life. One saying of his that I have heard makes this clear. "Unless the church travails," he would say, "the soul is not born."

The soul is the child of the body: at first that seems backwards. Surely the soul is the elder, even if we take "body" to mean "body of believers." The phrase seems backwards, I think, only because our notion of faith has become abstract and voluntary; we do not see faith as depending, for its very life, on the local body of worship and charity. We have watered down Simon Kreutziger's metaphor. Now the church is, or tries to be, a community. He had a more demanding, concrete and biblical sense of it.

It is not surprising, perhaps, that decades later he began to have trouble with his denomination, and ended his working life as a small contractor. His denomination took a fashionable tack, adopting full, instantaneous, individual sanctification in the Wesleyan mode. Simon Kreutziger could not be comfortable with that. I suspect (though I do not know) that it struck him as too private. He believed that it took the travail of the church to give even one soul birth. If there was going to be a sanctification, it would have to be another travail of the whole body, and a sanctification of the whole body.

The Spider's Web

These small northern Michigan churches constitute an urgent parable for American Christianity faced with the environmental crisis. They were small churches in small communities; and to compare them with our typical churches is to learn something about the general paralysis of our faith in the planet's peril—a paralysis brought on less by defective theology than by the church's enthusiastic assent to the breaking of living communities.

My grandfather's congregations were "gathered" churches. Their members had come by baptism into the "perfection of Christ." Pacifist and committed to gentleness, honesty and piety, they had marked themselves clearly out from secular society, which lived "under Caesar." They believed in the interpretation of Scripture within the circle of believers, in the cooperative committee structure for church work, in the bond of peace.

What is more important, these were churches bound together by their whole way of life—churches of small farmers and small tradesmen who shared work, the same woods and fields, the same skills, churches of intermarried families and close acquaintance. The substance of their fellowship was as much material as spiritual—even "tribal," as Donald Davie says. Before you took Communion, you faced the pastor and the rest of the church and affirmed that you had done nothing to "break the fellowship," a claim to be confirmed instantly, all around the circle of the people who knew you, like the shake on a spider's line.

These churches, then, were spiritual fellowships braced at all points on the concrete, particular, "worldly" life of their members. Their spiritual life had been brought out into the open. There is a profoundly important principle here: that charity is to be worked out in the immediate practical life of a known circle of people.

These people all did much the same work, with the same standards. One of their Mennonite ideals, like that of their theological cousins, the Amish, was "stewardship of the Lord's land." To be a good member of the community was to be a good steward of farmland, of the way of farming and therefore of the community's economic future. To be a bad member was not just to be a difficult church member. It might also be to be a bad—a destructive, lazy or greedy—steward of the common gift of God.

The criterion could work in reverse as well: being a bad farmer might threaten the fellowship into which you had been baptized. For bad farming—the industrial farming, for instance, that to survive must embody greed, adding (as Isaiah says) "field to field"—also destroys fellowship. It means, as Wendell Berry says, valuing your neighbor's farm over your neighbor.

The point is not, of course, that all good Mennonites were wise and careful farmers; or even that the careful farmers among them farmed in the best way. But the synthesis of ethical disciplines and spiritual privileges that made up the pattern of these churches included an ideal of *stewardship* that could not be violated without a corresponding violation of *fellowship.*

Not that these farmers thought in terms of "ecology" or "the environment" or "resources." We have fallen back on these inexact and abstract terms because few of us have any fields or woods to talk about. The older farmers farmed in the language of specific places: haying a particular field, buying stock of a known herd and farmer.

Their church language was religious—a language of vows, commitments, repentances, Christ and Caesar, the world and the body, sacrifices, offerings, graces and thanksgivings. But such words can be as precise as scientific language, when they refer to specific people in a small community. Such words also have great emotional power: they explain things, that is, and add to the explanation the power of love.

Half In and Half Out

Describing such a church makes it seem ideal; and the actual was, as it must always be, imperfect, narrow in its ways, partially completed. But saying this does not justify what has replaced it. The Mennonites on Ruttan Road constituted a body. That is, their life grew out of things held in common—a place, a practical and economic life, customs and skills, which made up the ground of their spiritual fellowship.

The question we must ask of every church and of every church project is this: What difference does the gospel make? The church must be tried by results—not only material ones, of course, but such spiritual results as make material differences. The life of the church moves from a mystery to the publication of that mystery—toward what everybody can see, plainly, in public. This is what it means to let your light shine.

I think it may be taken as true, if not obvious, that so far as the rampage of the technological culture through the creation is concerned, the gospel has not made much difference. Our churches are by and large paralyzed before the spectacle; they have endorsed the dominant culture, adopting its procedures and its way of thinking; they have failed to enact the relevant scriptural principles.

Yet it is crucial that they do so not just as a matter of spiritual health or doctrinal correctness. If my argument so far is granted in almost any degree, then we urgently need small, coherent bodies of conscientious people who will take responsibility for specific portions of the planet. Where will we find them if not among churches? Of course, Christians ought willingly to join any movement of conscience whose goals do not contradict the faith. But where should we look first for such a movement?

The reason for the church's paralysis has less to do with doctrine or moral intention than with the nature of the recent church as an institution. The crux is the split between spiritual and material lives. The institutional form of this split is that members of churches have already surrendered their practical lives to the technological culture before they walk through the church doors. The doctrine preached in church, consequently, may be scriptural, and even ecologically sensitive, and still make little genuine difference to our practical lives. That side of us is not present in church; which means that *we* are not present.

The problem belongs to the whole congregation as well as to the individual members. A building, a transportation program, mass-produced educational materials, a computer and a fax machine tie the church to the technological culture and therefore, inescapably, to its environmental costs.

Yet a church cannot simply do without organization and a social identity. It must organize its membership, find a way of making decisions in common, arrange for its worship; it must make public moral and spiritual judgments. The only way to avoid these needs is to deny that the church is material and cultural as well as spiritual, which would disable it from dissenting from its society.

A church begins to suffer for organization when it is no longer just the form of the church's communion and becomes an end in itself. This happens, I think inevitably, when the church becomes too large, and its members can no longer do for themselves. The social and economic life of the church is turned over, then, to the machines and "laws" of the surrounding culture. This has two practical effects: the church's social and financial life begins to be run on principles incompatible with the gospel, so that the church cannot oppose these principles without risking its own survival; and these principles begin to deform the church's sense of the gospel itself.

Repentance and Reconciliation

What happens then varies in place and time. Sometimes the church is simply swallowed by the national culture, becoming a political movement, as it has been in France, or it becomes a forthright and public support for the regime in place, as it was in England in the later eighteenth century and in Spain in the twentieth. The devastation of Spanish arable land by the *latifundia* system of enormous aristocratic estates and virtual slave labor was all accomplished with the blessing of the church.

In America we have vacillated, historically, between a "spiritual" gospel of individual redemption and millennial campaigns to remake the world. The first attracts us because we are individualists; the second attracts us because we believe in the mass distribution and consumption of ideas. Neither strategy will help us much in our present danger. Many people are converted without making any palpable change in their uses of energy; this does not strike us as a spiritual issue. But mass campaigns depend on the cheap energy of the technological culture. It is mass distribution and mass consumption, even of ideas, that are destroying us.

Eco-theologians such as Thomas Berry and Matthew Fox argue that doctrines of personal sin and repentance are distractions, now, from the "creation spirituality" that we need. In fact, however, we are in no position to do without these doctrines. Our systematic damage to the planet is a blazing example of our capacity for willing and doing what is evil.

The difficulty, in ecological terms, with the idea of personal redemption is not that it focuses our attention on our sins. The problem is that the range of these sins has been too narrow, and forgiveness offered on terms too cheap. We have confused the free offer of grace with an escape from responsibility—setting our guilt behind us with ignoring the harm we have done. But restitution means that part of repenting *is* attending to the harm that we have done. As far as the earth is concerned, we have a serious repentance to perform, and the restitution will be long, complicated, difficult, strenuous and expensive.

One requirement for this will have to be a firm grasp on an idea that we have never held on to for long—that reconciliation with God must be personal *and* communal, spiritual *and* material, not one without the other and not one more than the other. The results of the ministry of reconciliation must finally be changes in the way we live, practical changes, public, undramatic and permanent. This means building and then looking after a way of life, an economy, in which our spiritual growth is involved with the earthly work we have to do. The image of the church that we need is the image of a common life that leaves nothing essential out.

Common life: community. Here we are back with the Mennonites on Ruttan Road, and with the argument, from chapter five, that most of our communities are not really communities at all but (as Robert Bellah says) "voluntary associations." We hold onto community as a sort of shibboleth without being willing to submit to its requirements. But genuine community holds onto us; it grows out of common needs and the discipline of common practice. The most stable and powerful communities are those that answer, by the integrity of their common practices, the greatest number of needs.

Most of the life of church members does not occur in church. This would not matter, if the way taught in church had enough in common with the ways practiced outside. For most of our outside lives today, however, we are members in good standing of the consumer culture. We have turned over our practical needs to a system that has nothing in common with our circle of worshipers or the doctrine we hear. Someone we do not know feeds us, provides our shelter, clothing, light, heat, car, news, amusement and opinions. All of our practical needs lead out of the church and are governed by other values. No wonder the church strikes us as not of "the real world," otherworldly.

Even the preaching of the gospel, consequently, fails to have much braking effect on the consumer culture; nor can we look to it for guidance in preserving what the market is destroying. The only way to an effective Christian conscience on the environment is through freeing ourselves from the practices, and eventually the values, of the consumer culture.

What this means, ultimately, is taking back some immediate responsibility for our practical lives. We must begin to think, that is, not in terms of *freedom from needs,* but in terms of the *discipline of needs:* and we must begin to organize church communities that look after themselves and others practically as well as spiritually. Or, rather, we must realize that without the first the second is probably doomed to failure.

Large Family Churches
The small rural congregations of my grandfather's ministry understood this, though (strange as it sounds to say so) they did not know that they understood. What they knew was that they were responsible for their own material needs, and therefore for the skill, the good sense, the doctrine and the spiritual disciplines that this responsibility presupposed. Their practical lives taught them the mutual dependence that their spiritual health assumed.

Such churches no doubt still exist, even outside of the closed communities of the Amish. But they are obviously no longer the rule. The membership of the typical suburban church, liberal or evangelical, will be changeable and anonymous in comparison with the membership of the small rural church, in which several generations worshiped, and in which the members knew each other almost transparently. Many of the suburban church's members may not even know what other members do for a living; or, if they do, they recognize that the other professions mean other worlds of work and value in which they cannot participate. They regard each other from a great social and intellectual distance.

This is one symptom of the collision between the fellowship in the church and the culture that determines so much of its life. Two general responses to this strain exist; they are apparently different but actually much the same. One is the separatist impulse, which gives rise to intentional communities from which some aspects of the consumer culture can be excluded. The other is the response of the large suburban church, which can command large social and financial resources and use them for ambitious programs. The first seems inward-looking, the second outward-looking; the first seems quietist, the second activist.

Of course the large church must pay attention to fellowship. "We like to think of ourselves as a warm family church," a friend told me about her nondenominational congregation of five thousand. What the church substitutes for the community of needs and practices is a complicated network of church functions—clubs for age- and marriage-groups, coffee hours, Bible studies, sports leagues, children's and young people's fellowships, programs of extension work.

But these are all *church* work. They represent, not the reconciliation of life in and out of the church—not the hallowing of a common way of life—but the creation of another life in addition to the members' life outside of the church. The more energy the church program demands, the more time it takes up, the more clearly it is separated from "ordinary life"—from the jobs, employers, businesses and neighborhoods that split the congregation up again into its hundreds of separate worlds of experience.

The program, that is, is finally as separatist as that of the intentional religious community. The division comes at a different place: it comes within the member's life, not between it and "the world." It splits the life in half—half in church, half in the "real world" of the consumer culture.

Wherever the division comes theoretically, however, it threatens to disable the church's efforts to protest its culture. The congregations Bellah surveyed for *Habits of the Heart* (1985), liberal and evangelical, thought of the relation between church life and cultural life in terms of "outreach." But all of them have signed the cheap-energy contract and so lost their best chance of showing society a better way of living.

One lesson, for instance, of the fundamentalist political movement of the 1980s is that society easily absorbs and redirects such outreach. The fundamentalist church was too like the institutions of its society; it claimed to be an alternative, but its members made their livings, bought their food and advertised their convictions in the same way as everyone else. They thus perpetuated the sources of the moral confusion and political opportunism they cried out against.

The larger the church, moreover, the more this contradiction governs its life. The "ministry center" or "seeker center" of 15,000 members draws on the exploded community of the suburbs, stitched together with bus routes and commuter parking. The ministry makes enormous demands on transportation and fuel and on the latest communications technology. It is caught, ecologically speaking, in the same folly as the corporation, making increasing demands on a dwindling stock of fuel. Of course the seeker center makes small demands in comparison with GE. But then GE professes no spiritual or moral obligation to creation; and the church does, or ought to. But what does it represent through a practical life that consumes the creation more quickly with every member it enrolls?

The main tie, in such churches, between church life and society comes to be outreach in the form of witness, of soul-winning. The slogan you hear in many variations—"Come in to pray, go forth to serve"—states the problem with great clarity. There are two worlds, two directions, two ways to face. The common element is the individual church member. Yet however authentic her spiritual concern, however carefully she is trained in witnessing, the two worlds remain separate; in her law firm on Monday she is alone again, or at least belongs to another society than the one that on Sunday had seemed so warm a family.

Spiritual Electricity

Whatever this church's failings of koinonia, American Protestantism has a louder and more influential disciple of the cheap-energy culture in religious broadcasting and the electronic church. The means of this ministry are quite frankly the means of mass culture: state-of-the-art communications; mass mailings, packaging, sales technique and fundraising. Like other American social movements, the electronic church thinks in terms of international campaigns and crusades. The ideal is the invisible intercontinental network of the video image and the fax machine, or the impalpable touch of the television signal on the anonymous mind and wallet. It is the result of an almost agonized effort to remake faith in the image of cheap energy.

The urgent question about the electronic church is not ecclesiastical: not, for instance, Will it destroy the local church? The evidence suggests that it will not, just as mass evangelism neither destroyed the local church nor helped as much as the evangelists claimed. The question we need to ask is broader and deeper: What life-in-the-world does this ministry imply? The answer is that it sanctifies the cheap-energy culture by adopting its technology and its assumptions about how minds are to be changed—and by accepting, inevitably, what this culture costs to sustain it.

You cannot sell the gospel without making it into a saleable product; you cannot sell it on television without making it suitable to television. The medium is the message. This means that the gospel must become something simple, impersonal and compatible with the ideals of the consumer culture. The transformation is not due to the moral faults of evangelists (though their connivance with a destructive culture may itself be a fault). The gospel becomes a slogan because it must, if it is to be sold this way.

The gospel can, of course, be put into a sentence—"Jesus is Lord." But we must immediately ask, What does this mean, in practice? And the answer must be specific in place and time. The gospel's life in the world is infinitely particular, because it lives in the experience of people, in the complexities of their encounters with one another. A product, by contrast, is generalized and standard. It is offered for sale and use to (theoretically) everyone, and it must be such that it can be advertised and distributed with the greatest efficiency.

A gospel on this model can be marketed; but it can no more promise to sustain a common life in its market than a drug can dictate how it will be used, or a car how it will be driven. Despite feedback loops and banks of telephones, the electronic church is a one-way street. It sends messages; it can, to a degree, respond (with further formulas) to requests for help. But what it creates is not a community. It creates an audience— atomic, hypnotized (as the broadcasters themselves admit) by the screen image, with nothing in common but this image, and no concrete way to respond but by check.

The electronic church stands in the same relation to its audience as a business to its customers. It organizes, on their behalf, the distribution and even (to some extent) the production of a commodity. The customers use the commodity and respond with money; but apart from this they have no contact with each other. What they use the product for remains a matter of individual, isolated choice; and no common life, no mutual dependence, accountability or charity—the essential requirements of an earth-careful community—disciplines or enriches their actions.

Thus the electronic church endorses, and displays, the ways of a destructive economy. It cannot help endorsing them: it has been made in their image. Now through a computer service, called Sermonshop, ministers can ask an electronic network for help with their sermons. No doubt this increases their access to information. But it is a distortion nonetheless. Instead of a sermon fed and demanded by the church's common life and immediate needs, the minister offers a sermon built on advice from people he or she does not know, and who do not know the local congregation.

Simon Kreutziger used to say that he had never preached a sermon in his life. He brought messages. You see the difference. The second is immediate, personal, local. The messages were from a God he knew to people he knew. He was like a mailman who read all the letters he distributed. Of course he couldn't know what the letters meant to all the people, not unless they told him. But then in his small church, one way or another, they would.

Perhaps the most bizarre and revealing example of the cheap-energy gospel, however, is the well-known invitation of one evangelist to put your hands on the television as a way of joining the network of the Spirit. Thus the "magic of television" becomes literal magic. The power of the Spirit is identified with the power of transmission—with electricity, that industrial product which creates the picture on the screen.

But the power of the Spirit is, metaphors aside, nothing like electricity. It is not generated, as electricity is. It does not exist by the consumption of something else, oil, coal, nuclear ores; it does not exist, that is, by destruction. It is not abstract, but particular and immediate. It is not electricity but love, which grows and works without consuming or destroying, which heals without harm. And it will never run out.

As Many Churches as Valleys

The largest and oddest lie the cheap-energy culture tells us is that it is permanent. But the cheap energy will run out, perhaps relatively soon. The enormous tabernacles will go up for sale, along with the shopping malls; the parking lots will be empty, the cracking macadam that has poisoned the earth beneath it.

What will happen then, no one can say. But it may be a safe guess that the succeeding culture—perhaps, again, what Wes Jackson calls a "sunlight culture"—will be a smaller and quieter one than the one we know. So probably will be the church.

We will need to rebuild the structures of intensive fellowship. We will have to rediscover the grace of God, not as an industrial energy distributed by anonymous technicians across continents, but as a deep familiarity with each other and with the creation—as family-arity.

It is often commented that the early church, that model for all successive reformations, was "communist" in its economy. But we miss the ecological implications of this. The church practiced the holding of goods in common and the common distribution of necessities. Its practical life had to be just, charitable and responsible for its spiritual life to go on—and its prayers had to be genuine for its practical life to go on. The ecological maxim is: care for one another (the earth being a full member) or go hungry. It was the early church's maxim as well.

The lesson is not that we insert an arbitrary communism into the American church—especially not a Marxist communism with its recent history of totalitarianism and fear. The lesson is community—but genuine community, or body, that arises out of shared need and work.

Genuine communities differ from one another as people and places differ. The curse of cheap energy is standardization, flat, dictated homogeneity—so many Model Ts, as Ford said, all black. In the sunlight culture energy will be expensive again, and its supply will be local. This may teach us, again, to rely on our neighbors—teach us, again, the variety of communities.

We may learn then, too, that the gospel has as many lives as there are places and bodies of believers in them. We must stop talking about "the church" as a transcultural marshaling of resources. We must start thinking in terms of the believers on Ruttan Road. Their common life meant a different thing from that of the believers on the other side of the hill.

Among the 15,000 members of the seeker center there ought to be 150 churches—not one.

The gospel is universal in the same way nature is—universally health-giving and accessible, and yet different in every valley. There might be as many kinds of churches as kinds of apples. There would be one life and many gifts. Each community would travail until each soul was born—born out of the common life, and into it.

8
SEVERAL MILLION PROPHETS

WOULD THAT ALL THE LORD'S
PEOPLE WERE PROPHETS.

NUMBERS 11:29

A *little over fifteen years ago my wife and I began growing fruit* and vegetables for ourselves. Fifteen years of spades and stakes, mulch, weeds and compost; of rushing to get the garden in amid the hysterical busyness of the end of academic semesters; of catching our breath when the onions leap up and run along the surface of the ground like green flames.

We started out, a little vaguely, to be organic gardeners. Otherwise our notions of what we were getting into were limited. My wife had helped her mother garden and so knew more than I did. I had planted flowers and hewed sinks for bushes out of the stiff hill-country clay. Still I remember standing one spring morning in the modest weed-patch we meant to make into a garden, and wondering out loud how to get started.

My mother was standing nearby, and she answered me without a word. She reached for my hoe, stuck it into the weeds, flipped a small slab of sod over on its back and gave it that glancing whack that loosens soil from roots—the slight violence that starts the whole process, opening the earth to warmth and water, making the bacteria swarm. Then she handed the hoe back to me, still without speaking. That was how to start.

Know Thyself

The argument so far has been that the environmental crisis is not a natural phenomenon but a natural (and cultural) result of cultural choices; and that these choices embody moral and religious choices, the willingness, even eagerness, to live without obligation or community, an impatient contempt for created order. The cultural and moral center of the crisis means that scientific and technological knowledge, the knowledge of chemicals and machines, is not the knowledge we most need. What we need to understand is ourselves.

"Know thyself" was, of course, a commonplace in Western thinking from Athens to the Enlightenment. It is important to remember that the phrase was at first not a philosophical premise but practical advice. It was written over the door of Apollo's temple at Delphi, where the oracle (or prophetess) would give you, for a fee, a true answer to a single question. The catch was that the answer, interpreted by the priests of the temple, might be ambiguous; and further that you needed to know yourself accurately in order to use the answer safely—not to take it wrongly, or set off to act on it in ways that might be destructive.

The most famous response to an oracular answer was Socrates'; and his response illustrates a second fact about knowing yourself—it meant, by and large, knowing your limitations. The oracle's message, that no one in Athens was wiser than Socrates, meant (Socrates concluded) that human wisdom was in the end of little consequence, and that only the gods knew the truth of things.

Before the Industrial Revolution in the West, and even longer in subsistence cultures in other parts of the world, our cultural ways were designed to remind us to know ourselves—to know our limits; to acknowledge that God, or the gods, or the created order, alone held the truth about the cosmos and human existence in it. Our ways since 1800 have convinced us otherwise. Now we propel ourselves into the future on the presumption that a little technical information is enough to justify large-scale experiments on the fabric of life itself. But we can never know enough about circumstances to make such a presumption safe, or responsible. The only practical knowledge is the limits of what you know.

At root, knowing your limits is a religious matter. It means being aware that humanity has not chosen or defined its place in creation. But it would be naive to expect that we will regain an awareness of limits by going to church alone. In this culture even believers have two religions: the gospel that our cultural practices imply—the gospel of conquer and exploit—is not the one we profess to believe. And yet the power of the first gospel is so great, it fills so much of our daily horizon, that if it does not supplant Christianity it does clog, deform and misdirect it.

We thank God for our material prosperity and pray for more of the same. But this prosperity means disaster to the natural world and suffering to our human sisters and brothers. Seen from the Third World, our prayers are the kind that bombs and plagues would make.

In addition to reminding ourselves of the obligations implicit in the Christian gospel, then, we need evidence for, and about, better cultural practices—evidence to persuade us that they are possible, that the technological culture is not the only way to handle the practical requirements of human life; evidence of what these practices look like and of how to perform them.

It will not be hard for us to reacquaint ourselves with nature. Nature stands at our elbows. We can start our reacquaintance with it almost as we would start with another person. We can turn and look at the tree next door—really look at it; learn its name; find out what work it does. We can begin whenever we choose—whenever gratitude and curiosity get the better of greed and laziness.

The search for better cultural options is not so easy. The difficulty, plainly, is that we are so wound in our present habits that other options seem unimaginable. So where do we begin to look?

Looking Back

There is a true and simple answer: to the past. This is not only, however, a simple answer; it is a risky one, dangerous to offer, hard to hear. Someone will object, instantly, that we cannot go back in time, and in a physical sense this is true. (It does not follow that we cannot readopt selected practices from the past.) Literally speaking, we have nowhere to go but into the future.

But going there is not like driving down a familiar road to a known destination. It is more like sitting at the controls of a racing train and not knowing what button to push. If we are on the wrong track—and it seems undeniable that we are—we can hardly expect to get somewhere desirable by simply continuing. We must find a map by which to judge the route we are taking.

The technological culture exaggerates the built-in uncertainties of living in time. It specializes, as we said in chapter six, in change too rapid to adapt to; it is always shoving us toward the next invention or break-through; and in two hundred breakneck years we have not learned to be wary of its claims. Its philosophy is historicist, which means that it believes in the inevitable good evolution of culture from "primitive" to "advanced" and beyond, from the fresh carrot to the precooked prepackaged microwavable carrot-chip. To look back for wisdom seems like nonsense.

Of course there is a superficial appeal to the past. However fond we are of the Norman Rockwell Vermont-calendar "past," we are right to be suspicious of it as a guide to thinking. Its gnatless swimming holes and carefully antiqued faces are a lie about actual life in any time or place.

We ought to notice, though, that such images are almost always the property of some political or financial interest. The technological culture, railroading us into the future, has a use for the past: it turns the past into a cartoon, which can be used to sell beer or movies but which, because it is not truthful, cannot be used to measure our ambitions or our losses. Pancake syrup is always "old-fashioned"; it is often sold with attractive pictures of sap-gathering in the New England woods. But the syrup owes nothing to maple trees; and the synthetic product threatens the maple farmer's livelihood. So this "past" is a lie with intent to harm.

The typical academic reaction to such images is equally superficial and self-serving. Cultural historians routinely deny that coherent, organic or rational subsistence cultures ever existed; or, alternatively, that they were any less unhappy, confused and destructive than our own. The denial is, historically speaking, demonstrably wrong. Yet we are as much historicists in our classrooms as in our boardrooms. We want our thinking to be as up-to-date and sourceless as are our computers. And the modern university was born out of and lives, on a day-to-day basis, on the profits of the cheap-energy culture. Asking the university to criticize this culture more than indirectly is asking the creature to turn on Dr. Frankenstein.

The result is that we do not know how to use our knowledge of the past. Indeed we wonder if it has any uses; or if we have any such knowledge; or even if, supposing we do, we might be obligated to sabotage or deny it. Yet systematic memory is (apart from revelation) the only map we have for judging our route into the future. How the past is to be fruitfully connected with plans for the future is a question of enormous intellectual and practical importance—and one, it seems to me, for which we have no good answers.

The dishonesty of idealizing subsistence cultures, and our genuine need to learn from them, have both been succinctly stated by George Ewart Evans, the British agricultural historian:

No thinking person would advocate the return of the old domination [of English country life] by squire or near-squire that most villages have suffered in the past. But the fact has to be met that the community was organic, at however low a level; and since its fragmentation village life, and therefore the life of the nation, has suffered because nothing comparable has taken its place.

Nothing comparable has taken its place: this is the crux of the matter. The socially coherent community whose shared beliefs can be enacted in a sustained cultural practice is, or was, a staple of human life; because it makes possible a long tenure in a given place, it is probably a fundamental requirement of human life. But what has replaced it is neither coherent nor sustainable: people organized not into communities but into markets, without sustained cultural practice, with tools constantly becoming obsolete and with beliefs shrunken into lifestyles. The tyranny of the squire was bad; that of the corporation—because it knows no limits, technical or moral—is infinitely worse.

An honest and humble appeal to the past does not mean trying to submit ourselves to all of its conditions. It does not mean, for instance, halting all further scientific or technological work. We need new technical solutions to specific problems. I would give a lot for an efficient home solar system under ten thousand dollars. Wes Jackson's profoundly important research in foodstuff polyculture depends on new biological research.

But such solutions (as Jackson is the first to say) are, in a sense, incidental to the crisis. Its fundamental predicament is moral; and no new moralities exist. A technical change may produce a new case for moral consideration; it does not produce a new morality. Nuclear weapons did not give the commandment against murder any greater force, or drain any of its force away. They just deepened the horror of our disobedience.

The moral principles for working our way out of the environmental crisis are already familiar; and there have been communities where these principles were at least more fully in evidence than in ours; yet these communities are largely in or from the past. Now we have to fight our way back to them.

Neighboring a Community

We have to fight, however, not because the past is so far away, but because the present is so noisy. The past is not in the past; it is all around us.

I doubt if we realize how quickly the crisis of planetary life has come on us. Suppose we dated events not from the birth of Christ but (less hypocritically, perhaps) from the birth of the technological culture. If we made 1765 the year one—it was the year James Watt began to perfect the steam engine—then the Declaration of Independence was signed in the year 11 A.W. (After Watt). Slavery, mostly for agricultural purposes, was legal in the United States until 98. The first Model T appeared in 143, the first supermarket in 148. The first working computer was wired up in 179; Hiroshima vanished in 180. This page was written in 227. It is still early in the new epoch. Think how fast the damage has been done.

Think how close we are, however, to the older world. Two generations separate me from Lincoln. The lives of three people, end to end, would reach back to Watt. The past is not in the past.

The scattered communities of unanimous cultures still exist, in states of greater or lesser shock, all over the globe: farming villages on the Indian subcontinent, rice-growing communes in Bali, tribal communities in the Philippines and Amazonia, peasant villages in South America, nomadic pastoralists in Africa. Even in postindustrial North America we are not quite out of touch with them. There are overt religious communities of Old Order Amish, Hutterite and Bruderhof. Native Americans cling gingerly to the skirts of the technological culture, trying to preserve or resurrect their own traditions. A few of us still live in farming or fishing communities that retain some continuity with their own pasts in a shared knowledge of places and customs. A few more of us have contact with such communities through the living memories of aged relatives and friends.

But most of us live in exile. This is the meaning of a "mobile" culture, even (or especially) if the mobility is upward. Nor can the intact communities take us in again. The Amish are largely closed to entrance from the outside—certainly from mass entrance. In our perpetual agricultural depression, the best they can offer us, the model of a renewed and sensitive farming, is itself under siege. Older regional communities go on dwindling under the relentless efforts of government, corporations and education to drag the young away.

The opportunities for learning from such a community directly, therefore, are slim. They are worth mentioning, however, because the best ecological instructions come from people who enact them. These instructions are less like doctrines than they are like stories, like gossip. They represent whatever beliefs the community consciously holds incarnate in a body of practice—or practice instinct with belief.

They come, that is, as wisdom, as aptitude, as cunning, as loyalties and attachments. They take many forms: knowledge of resources and skills, including the knowledge of who knows, of the sources of information; knowledge of who does work best and who cannot be trusted; knowledge of the immediate countryside and climate, in detail; local history, personal and family biography; memories of work and extraordinary accomplishments; memories of failed experiments and wrong measures; stories, fables, tall tales. It is wisdom that can plant a row; wisdom that knows which tree to cut and which to leave alone.

The advantages of learning one's ecological principles in a community of skillful and sensible people are equally obvious and enormous. Most of us, however, belong to no such community; we may not know where to find one; we might not notice that one exists in the vicinity. The best possibility for us, then, is to find and neighbor one, if we can—not appropriate it, or presume to insert ourselves into it on demand, or even presume that we can be its champions. *Neighbor* it: this means, first, to talk with its members, or with the people who remember it. It may be possible to fuse their knowledge of a place with ours, to flesh out the landscape with their experience of it. It may be possible to work with them, or for them, or to accept their help.

It is impossible to say, in general, what such neighboring of a community-in-place would amount to. The goal is not general knowledge but particular. Such a relationship may never work itself free of a certain embarrassment or artificiality. We may never feel at home: this is the price we pay for our folly in destroying the social and political basis for such community among us. Neighbors of this kind are always strangers—though a community-in-place is often more generous about its resources and ways than we expect it to be. It can afford to be generous, however limited its physical resources. It knows who and what it is, and what it expects of itself. Generosity is the fruit of spiritual repose.

Books for Grandparents
Eighty years ago Liberty Hyde Bailey wrote that it ought to be one "fundamental purpose" of American education "to acquaint the people with the common resources of the region [where they live] and particularly with those materials on which we subsist." A required general education course, that is, in local flora and fauna, especially those good for food and fuel, to be taken along with Western Civilization and Ethics 101. That such a requirement would seem absurd to most American schools is the result of at least two things: the students of a typical college have no region in common, and those of a typical high school will disperse as soon as they can; and American education assumes that the problems of subsistence are purely technical, and therefore not the concern of the educated public at large.

But for most of us, making up our losses in community and ecological good sense is going to mean education in a fairly specific sense—that is, reading books. *"Books are our grandparents!"* says Gary Snyder: they are our replacement, that is, for the accurate wisdom of living people; a replacement with greater range, but with less precision and less warmth.

It is logical to look for information about subsistence cultures in history and anthropology. Conventional history, concentrating on battles, treaties, monarchs and parliaments, tended for a long time to shove the issues of subsistence aside. Only when the captains and the kings went back into their dressing rooms did we get chapters on "background"—agriculture, that is, modes of provision and ordinary economic life, "the place of women," the nurture of children, religion and custom. Such chapters were backdrop thinking with a vengeance.

For the truth is that how we ate, married, raised children, farmed and built houses, barns and estates has always been the substance of life for most human beings, and therefore (one might think) the essential and telling dimension of history. But it is only relatively recently that academic history has concurred. The early work of scholars such as Dorothy George, J. L. and Barbara Hammond, and E. P. Thompson has made possible efforts, such as Peter Laslett's frequently updated *The World We Have Lost* (first edition 1965), to reconstruct preindustrial life. Fernand Braudel's enormous survey, *Civilization and Capitalism, 15th Century to 18th Century* (1979-1984), is a reservoir of information about the life that preceded, and prepared for, the great transformation.

"Landscape history" takes similar kinds of information as clues to how we have formed specific parts of the earth; the work of J. B. Jackson, David Sopher and D. W. Meinig, and John Stilgoe's wonderful *Common Landscape of America* (1982) are examples. Many studies exist of specific agrarian communities, such as John Hostetler's of the Amish (Hostetler grew up Amish) and E. D. Andrews's and Priscilla Brewer's of the Shakers. Finally, there is "ecological history" proper, such as A. W. Crosby's *Ecological Imperialism* (1986), a study of the spread of European plants and animals into other parts of the globe.

An enormous amount of information exists about traditional communities in what we call the Third World, but it is of mixed value for a reader with environmental concerns. Anthropologists have come to a time of reproaching themselves, sometimes violently, for "ethnocentrism." And it is true that anthropology has always been, to some extent, the story of disappearing cultures told by the culture that was undermining them. Still, both primitive and advanced cultures need wisdom in matters of subsistence—environmental matters, that is—and the cruel difficulties of "translating" cultures (to use Clifford Geertz's term) can be lessened by admitting this common need. That a humble and practical anthropology can be written—with gains of usable ecological wisdom—is shown by a work such as Richard Nelson's *Make Prayers to the Raven* (1983), a study of the Athapaskan Koyokuk people.

The real danger comes less from academic anthropology than from its popular versions, which also present themselves as sources of wisdom and which are valued, often for religious uses, by environmentally inclined readers. The difficulty with the fad of shaman studies begun by Carlos Castaneda, for instance, is that we cannot simply airlift a Hopi wisdom into mainstream postindustrial culture for whatever good we can get out of it. Such wisdom was particular, community-specific; it belonged to a place and a tradition. At best, we cheapen and dilute it by packing it into bestsellers; at worst, we mislead ourselves with false religious options, or make complex religious questions into postures and poses.

A genre somewhere between landscape history and autobiography may, in the end, be the most useful to us who are far from the land and its communities. This genre is sometimes called the "literature of place." Its American roots are certainly in Thoreau, and in his followers, such as John Muir and Mary Austin. But dozens of recent examples are written by people who have grown up in, or adopted, a geographical region and come to know it over decades, or a lifetime, of experience: Wendell Berry's northern Kentucky and Gary Snyder's Sierras are familiar to people who will never visit them. These landscapes come to make moral claims on us. John Haines has written wonderfully of his Alaskan homesteading; Gretel Ehrlich of rural Wyoming, Ronald Jager of western Michigan, David Kline of Amish Ohio, Donald Hall of New England and John Leax of rural New York.

Finally, there is a form of direct personal testimony that ought not to be ignored. This includes the less analytical form of history called "oral history," which collects records of traditional customs from those who remember them; it may be represented by Eliot Wigginton's long series of *Foxfire* books about southern Appalachia. One advantage of such records is that they can be made by anyone with an older neighbor or relative willing to reminisce. It would be better to preserve such history in the active memory of a working community than to put it in a book; but it is better to put it in a book than to let it disappear.

The Crank in the Woods

Among the books we can turn to for help are a few that are not merely sources of information. They are rather testimonies, books that began with and record experiments in living, and that hope to influence living. One writer of such books, who has been cited often in these pages, is the American farmer and poet Wendell Berry. We will come back to him in a moment. But the most important such book for American environmentalism is doubtless Henry David Thoreau's *Walden: Or, Life in the Woods.*

Thoreau's move to the shore of Walden Pond in the spring of 1845 is another moment, like the Wordsworths' move to Grasmere, that has come to have extraordinary, almost mythical power. Depending on how you look at it, the hut by the pond is a pattern for all successive moral protest against industrial civilization, or the act of a cranky solitary who refused to recognize the facts when he saw them.

Henry Thoreau was undoubtedly an odd and self-centered man (though his range of friends and his kindness to them were greater than we normally suppose). He was undoubtedly cranky; and yet, as some artists do, he made deliberate use of his idiosyncrasies. He made his life an experiment for his thought; he stood clearly apart from his Concord neighbors so that they could see him clearly. "It would be some advantage," he wrote early in *Walden,* "to live a primitive and frontier life, though in the midst of an outward civilization, if only to learn what are the gross necessaries of life and what methods have been taken to obtain them." A frontier life, then, meant a life on the boundaries, where he could be seen testing and analyzing the "methods" of his society where it abutted on "the necessaries of life."

What this means is that Thoreau was (as Robert Frost said of himself) "not undesigning." This will seem a loss only if we expect to find in *Walden* a siren song about "escape" into nature—the impulse that drives motorcycles into the national parks on California weekends. This is not, however, what we find; and it is not what we need. What we find is a complex and testy experiment in *living with nature*—that is to say, in *culture*.

Walden's first, longest chapter is called "Economy," and while Thoreau certainly means by this moral and spiritual economies, he also means simple practical economics, dollars and cents, getting and spending. Thoreau's Concord was in the midst of a transition between an older subsistence farming and a newer market-based economy; and part of his experiment is intended to test the advantages that were being claimed for the change. Of course we need somewhere to live: but do we need to be "crushed and smothered" by our possessions? Does a farmer have to live with the enormous investments of farming for the market?

Thoreau's elaborate parody of Benjamin Franklin's moral accounting—so many dollars for shingles, ten cents for a latch, a penny for chalk—is meant to bring the obsession with money back to earth: "the cost of a thing is the amount of what I will call life which is required to be exchanged for it." By this standard the economics of Concord were upside down: "The farmer is endeavoring to solve the problem of livelihood by a formula more complicated than the problem itself. To get his shoestrings he speculates in herds of cattle." The result is a waste of real, moral life, and the ruin both of farmers and of their community.

Walden is full, of course, of Thoreau's love of solitude. When nature and the solitary come together the effect can be intoxicating: "To anticipate, not the sunrise and the dawn merely, but, if possible, Nature herself! How many mornings, summer and winter, before any neighbor was stirring about his business, have I been about mine!"

For all their exuberance, however, such passages do not make

Walden into a "nature book." It is rather a testament about culture-in-nature, tested in the one life Thoreau had to experiment with. His living "sturdy and Spartan-like" to find out his own "necessaries" was meant to show communities that they needed a similar discipline:

> The nation itself, with all its so called internal improvements, which, by the way, are all external and superficial, is just such an unwieldy and overgrown establishment, cluttered with furniture . . . and heedless expense, by want of calculation and a worthy aim, as the million households in the land; and the only cure for it as well as for them is a rigid economy, a stern and more than Spartan simplicity of life.

It might be said that a rigid economy and a Spartan simplicity are precisely what our generations of consumption and waste are making necessary.

Thoreau was not a Christian. Still Donald Worster's claim that Thoreau's importance to environmentalism lies in his paganism strikes the wrong note, at least for *Walden*. Among his sometimes admiring, sometimes teasing references to pagan myth and Sanskrit scripture, Thoreau was bent on testing religious principles by performance. Not a good criterion for Scripture itself, perhaps: but a good one for Concord's Christianity. The frequent biblical quotation in *Walden* is there to show how consistently and systematically Concord failed to live up to its professions. Yet Thoreau's own moral mottoes are sometimes surprisingly close to the New Testament pattern: "Rescue the drowning and tie your shoelaces." Compare "Do not let your left hand know what your right is doing." Concord was too proud of being Christian to be Christian in the matter of its shoelaces: and as a consequence it was itself drowning.

There and Back Again

Thoreau was the author of one book, essentially—one book and one essay ("Civil Disobedience"). Wendell Berry has written more than twenty-five books so far, with promise of more to come, including several collections of essays and poems, four novels and two volumes of short stories. Since the publication of *The Unsettling of America* in 1977 he has been an inescapable presence in the environmental movement and specifically in the defense of traditional farming.

Berry inherited his cause, in a sense, when he chose to root his writing in the northern Kentucky region where he had been born. Except for a few minor excursions Thoreau stayed home all of his life. Berry's career has had two movements, away and returning. Having begun to teach and publish in New York, he came back to Kentucky in 1963, at first to live, and then to farm, within a few hundred yards of family land. Later he would rewrite Frost's poetic invitation, "You come too," to read:

I am at home. Don't come with me.

You stay home too.

But the lesson of Berry's work, within the American unsettling, has been more like "I went home; you go home too."

Which is to say, among other things, that though Berry is correctly associated with the defense of traditional farming, his message is certainly not that everyone should be a farmer, any more than Thoreau's was that everyone should be a pondside hermit. Berry is an advocate of placedness ("whereas most American writers—and even most Americans—of my time are displaced persons, I am a placed person"), but the places of American life are legion, and responsible care can and must be taken of all of them. The principle is global as well: " 'The problem of world hunger' cannot be solved until it is understood and dealt with by local people as a multitude of local problems of ecology, agriculture, and culture."

But "place" in Berry's thinking is more than physical; and here we meet one reason why his work is so important for environmental thinking as a whole. "Place" means something like "community-in-place-and-time." The place has been made as well as found, by people whose uses of the land have given them a mutual history—so that the history of the people is a history of land, and vice versa. This is a community of homes, of animals domestic and wild, of forest, watershed and river, of fields and seasons of work; a community of belief, memory, cumulative awareness of natural circumstances and of what people can and ought to do. Finally, "place" is a metaphysical condition. To know where you belong, in terms of a specific landscape, is to fit in your place in creation.

Part of this place, then, is belief, which allows for a correct understanding of the place. Berry's community is traditionally Christian, and for his work the Scriptures are normative. While he has been often critical of the American church for a false otherworldliness and for abandoning rural places and people, Berry has also taught the practicality of faith—not that faith is justified by its usefulness, but that right belief has its results in safe action. His 1979 essay "The Gift of Good Land" builds a "Biblical argument for ecological and agricultural responsibility." It is an intelligent and practical answer to people who assume, often thoughtlessly, that Christianity is the enemy of environmental concern.

How religion is to reach matters so specific as the care of a given valley is obviously a question; and Berry's answer is again a major help to our thinking. All human activity, he says more than once, is carried on within a series of concentric households—nature, culture, community, family—and any action must be judged with reference to the health of these households. Infidelity in the family makes disorder in the community, whose task is to maintain cultural ways and look after the land. A culture—to go the other way—that turns its back on nature and is in love with abstractions like money will tear its communities apart and encourage families to dissolve. No cultural action—no action at all—can be judged outside its households.

There is a danger of misunderstanding, however, in talking about Berry's work in such generalizations. For his work has always been *in particular*: a given valley, a given group of people, particular skills and affections. The literary form of this particular devotion is that much of his writing has not been essay or argument but poetry and fiction—concrete imaginings.

> I came to
> a farm, some of it unreachable

by machines, as some of the world
will always be. And so
I came to a team, a pair
of mares—sorrels, with white
tails and manes, beautiful!—
to keep my sloping fields.

Berry's poems are unusual in recent American poetry in that they are often forthrightly didactic and controversial—such as his "Manifesto: The Mad Farmer Liberation Front," which Berry read at Edward Abbey's funeral and which has become a kind of marching song for many environmentalists. But Berry's characteristic form is the meditative lyric, dignified, generous:

I come into the peace of wild things
who do not tax their lives with forethought
of grief. I come into the presence of still water.
And I feel above me the day-blind stars
waiting with their light. For a time
I rest in the grace of the world, and am free.

Berry's novels and stories center around the fictional community of Port William, Kentucky, and a web of related friends and families. We follow the families through generations, and yet the stories are not the typical bestselling melodramas of generational struggle and betrayal. Port William is one of the few sustained and coherent communities in American fiction—perhaps the only one in which the characters feel, enact and state the ideals by which they live. Port William is to this extent an ideal community, though normally not idealized, and consequently is Berry's tribute to the community whose argument with the technological culture he took up thirty years ago.

Prophets
There is a temptation in all of this writing, however, which a good many so-called environmentalists succumb to, and not always reluctantly. It is

to turn a cause into a matter of information. Being an environmentalist ends up being someone who reads environmentalist books—someone with the right opinions and vocabulary, someone who talks in terms of "lifestyles" and "resources," someone who networks with environmental lobbies and sends a check to the lobby of choice. Someone in danger, that is, of missing the point altogether.

For no information is properly an end in itself, and no practical book exists only to be read. It exists to help; and what we need help with is living. An environmentalist is not someone who reads a certain kind of book, but someone who lives in a certain way—or who is engaged in working out, in terms of daily practice, what the right way is in the present circumstances. By daily practice I mean eating, dressing, heating the house, driving the car, planting the yard. And the best teachers—if you can find them—are not people who write books but people who know how to dress a garden and preserve food.

There is a biblical principle here, I think—the diffusion of spiritual understanding through the body of believers. It is stated most memorably, for me at least, in Moses' cry, "Would that all the Lord's people were prophets!" This does not mean, I take it, that everyone has the same gift of prophecy in the technical sense, or even of our watered-down versions of it, such as writing books. It means that each member of a community may teach the wisdom of that community in her actions. To do good work is to prophesy. To know the best way to produce, store, distribute and prepare food—the very skills we pride ourselves on having left behind—would be to be an environmental prophet; it would be to circulate the best ecological wisdom. A community of prophets might mean, in our desperate times, a community of people whose cultural practice is earth-careful, efficient and full of gratitude.

9
The
SHELTER
and the
FIELD

YET HAVE I FIERCE AFFECTIONS.

WILLIAM SHAKESPEARE

ow, to solutions.

It is not hard to name some. You can buy any one of a dozen books on the model of "One Hundred Things You Can Do," and many of the suggestions will be practical and doable. You can buy compact fluorescents for the important lamps in your home, and recycle your pop cans. Writing a letter to the CEO of Xerox may seem a little like writing to one of Jupiter's moons. But you can learn to build a composter for your leaves.

But we are in a curious, and dangerous, moment in the environmental crisis. It is now, at last, a popular thing to care about the environment. It is a political advantage; business is greening itself, or its image, in search of commercial advantages. At the same time, politics and business continue to pump the adrenaline of "growth economics." Our forests are falling faster than ever, and poverty and hunger swarm more desperately every year, on every continent.

In this unsettling slippage between convictions (or professed convictions) and results, a fashionable or merely pragmatic environmentalism will not be enough. I have insisted now, for eight chapters, that the crux of our ecological situation is practice. Now it is time to say that the practices we need will be ones that teach us to change our minds.

Let us be clear about this: the danger in which we stand is a result of spiritual and moral failures as well as of practical foolishness. We do, as the authors of *Earthkeeping* (1980) have written, need a change of "world model," a conversion of our "hidden mind." The question is how this is to be done; for I doubt that a world model, of the kind that sees the world (for instance) as a machine, can be changed by taking thought. The only hope lies, I think, in taking up different practices—work, that is, that will change our minds.

The question facing us is not, therefore, What can we do? The question is, What should we do (and what should our culture do) in order to learn how to limit our appetites, how to doubt our capacities, how to wait on the creation?

Doubt Thyself

The fundamental criteria for a new practice are all forms of humility. First is the humility of program. We ought to do things for which we can, in great measure, be directly responsible; we ought to do things that will change our daily lives and those of our families and neighbors.

This may seem irresponsible in the face of humanity's problems. Global warming, or the fate of a billion Third World people without adequate sanitation or water, makes backyard solutions seem stingy and self-absorbed. Remember, however, what we are looking for: work that we, American believers, can do to change our minds. The big problems will be unmet, and unrecognized, until we can persuade ourselves to want a different way of life. And this persuasion starts at home.

Both anxiety and optimism will tell us that our first need is huge governmental programs and international finance. This is part of the American creed: big solutions for big problems; no problem too big. This is the incessant refrain of recent politics, and one reason why it seems to be carried on more and more in fantasy. The truth is that we can no longer afford big solutions. We need, rather, to model and share an American modesty. This is one form our repentance for greed and selfishness might take.

It is not only a matter of repentance, however, but of hope. We need sources of hope, and they must be palpable, hope we have a hand in. They must be standing proof to us that we can do what we must. They must therefore be something particular, specific and close to hand.

Second, there is a humility of means. Big solutions are designed in terms of large means—the Aswan Dam, the Colorado River flood project, space colonies orbiting the moon. But we are coming to a time when we no longer have the energy or the money for large means, or for correcting the harm that they do. We need inexpensive solutions with many good results. Such a technology would fit our needs into natural movements and placements of energy; it would take advantage of what nature will do in any case.

Third, and hardest to talk about, we must judge by humility of mind. Probably I need to say nothing further about the presumption of the technological culture. But we must be careful that our criticism of the arrogance and abstraction of this culture does not become arrogant and abstract itself.

As various as the environmental movement is—third-wave farmers, solar scientists, wilderness activists, grassroots political organizers, handicrafters, worshipers of a variety of gods and goddesses—we are in danger of coming to worship, as well, our own definitions. Our minds are already barnacled with clichés: *resources, stewardship, genocide* and *ecocide, corporate America,* even *wilderness.* You have read some of these terms in this book. But they are not, at basis, the words of the crisis or of its solution. They are the words of our unconvinced and abstract approaches to the crisis.

What are the words of the solution? They sound like this: *boots, dirt, watershed, beetle, tomato, compost, rot, stink* and *shovel*. These are words of proper scale and proper means. For "serving justice" substitute "feeding"; for "community" substitute "Chet" and "the Smiths down the block." For "nature" substitute "backyard."

What Will Not Work

If we measure by these humilities, I think we see fairly quickly that certain popular nostrums will not help us much.

We cannot expect business to "green" itself and then to save the world. It may help to look at an example of greening. I have beside me an oil company's quarterly report, which announces an $85,000 grant for preserving long-grass prairie. The subtext of this item is clear: this is what you want; this is what we provide.

How much, however, did the corporation spend on finding new sources of oil, with all the attendant results—the opening of rainforest, the disturbances of sea life, the constant threat, constantly realized, of damage from spills, the encouragement of our obsession with this form of energy, poisonous as it is, addictive and hot? I do not know how much the corporation spent; but any imaginable amount is so much greater than $85,000 that the grant simply vanishes. The hypocrisy of the grant, however, is not in the intentions of the corporation's employees or stockholders. It is inextricable from the corporation as a thing with one overriding purpose, to pay dividends. The corporation cannot, by its nature, do anything or stop doing anything on any other grounds. To ask it to stop drilling for love of the planet—or even for love of the planet's people—is to ask something it cannot comprehend. You are talking to it in a mysterious language, the Xhosa or Inuit of morality. The only language it knows is profit.

Nor will greening the consumer market save us. Ultimately, what we make and buy will have to change along with what we think and hope for. At the moment, however, a simple lifestyle does not threaten consumerism, as long as the market can supply its bicycles and green cotton shirts. The goal of the market is not an intact community or the health of the earth. It is still profit. The moment another fashion replaces the green fashion, the market will veer off after it. It cannot do otherwise.

Nor will the government save us. Political changes must and will come. But our political idolatry of "the economy," especially when production is slow and jobs are lost, makes government largely subordinate to business. And business will earn its privileges by doing the government's work where political goals seem to be at stake: the corporations that poisoned earth and water with radioactive waste while they made the materials for nuclear weapons have every excuse for the harm they did, so far as the government is concerned.

We cannot, finally, expect large environmental lobbies to win the day for us. Apart from the fact that the largest and most vocal of them, such as the Sierra Club, openly endorse the growth economy, it is too easy to substitute a check to the lobbyist for local work. The larger the organization, the more generalized its projects, the more it depends on corporate strategies (and corporations) to accomplish them. We do, of course, need organizations that can publicize large infringements on wilderness preserves and national forests. What we need even more, however, is responsible work on small, local projects.

The Marrow of the Thing

I remarked in the introduction that this book has been written in my car, in the garden and on the dining-room table. A good deal of it has been written, in addition, on a small picnic table on the back porch. The table is made of unfinished Wolmanized lumber, warping (despite the waterproofing) in the fearsome damps of Michigan summers. I work looking out across yard and garden to the small pocket of wetlands and the wooded hills beyond that: I have to weight my papers with stones and driftwood. Sometimes the mosquitoes get the better of inspiration and I go inside. Sometimes inspiration is swallowed up in looking.

People have an old habit of thinking of cities as the hubs of the countryside, so that driving to the city means coming "in" and driving to the country means going "out." Since we live fifteen miles from the city, on the leftovers of a farm, people often ask us how things are "out there." The implication seems to be that we live a block from the Milky Way, and that for so strange an undertaking there must be powerful reasons.

There is a sense in which this book is my reasons. I did not come "out here" to write it. But if we had not come "out here," I suspect that I would feel that I had no right to be writing it. No matter that our efforts at going free of a destructive, totalitarian economy are modest—a raspberry patch, a woodstove, shelves of pickles and jams. In a sense, doing much is not necessary. It is necessary to do something—only preferable to do much. The something that you do gives you a place to stand.

Not that you cannot make a stand in the city. The heroes of San Francisco put recycling into the American mind. Nancy and John Todd's New Alchemy Institute envisions sidewalk gardening and old factories made into "solar food barns." But city living hardly encourages such things. The point about the modern city is that you can live autonomously, if you want—without community, with no more than minimal practical obligations—and have the system work for you. If you desire to live in this way, you are not likely to want a garden and a woodstove. They are inconvenient; they tie you down; they maximize obligations.

This is, of course, their value. They are small instances of the great human problem of fitting culture to nature. The technological culture began as an attempt to solve this problem. But it has proceeded for a long time now on the theory that we can transcend the problem. This is a fallacy. The energy, machines and politics of transcending the problem have harmed the planet.

We need to get back to the problem itself: that is, to feel it again as a problem—or rather as an unavoidable task to be carried on. One way to feel this again is to make yourself responsible, in part, for your own subsistence; directly responsible for some small piece of the earth.

There are at least two dangers in the project; or rather it allows for two misconceptions. The first is to see it as an exercise in escapism. So Thoreau and Berry have been seen as turning away from the true location of society's evils, the city, the self-conscious kingdoms of politics and finance. It would be more accurate to say that they turned away from society's solutions. To take some measure of responsibility for your life in nature, so as to change your mind, is not an escape; it is a form of attention. My plot of ground adjoins yours; we are neighbors. We are all harvesting or poisoning the same planet under the same rules. But if I am not paying attention to my ten acres, then I am not really paying the proper, required attention to anything, and consequently I will never learn the rules.

The other misconception is a sort of opposite of the first: it is to expect the wrong kind of benefit. Sentimental writers (like the worshipers of Gaea) tell us that we can expect to find God in our gardens, and spiritual peace and harmony with all creation, and so on. But a real garden will have mostly other things in it: dirt, plants (wanted and otherwise), insects, fungus, rot and worms; hard work, discouragement, anger and impatience. There will be too much rain or too little, too much heat or cold, and the woodchuck will get the broccoli.

You will not find God in the garden unless you can also find him in a shopping mall. He will not fit into our dreams of Eden. One of his purposes is constantly to remind us (as Milton said) of "our loss of Eden."

Our sentimental gardens, our cheap and false Edens, are far too close to our desires. They can be bought from a catalog, like a kit or a package tour; you can hire a landscaping firm to create and maintain them. They will not give us what we need—the rough walls and stony going of our actual spiritual condition, so that we may fall and feel our fall, and skin our knees and hands. A real garden will do this for you.

It may also give you great pleasure and help to feed you. There is no reason a repentance cannot eventuate in beans.

Eight Suggestions

This is how we will learn: thousands of people looking after thousands of small tracts of land, in the sweat of their brows and with whatever counsel and help they can find in their neighborhoods. It is hard to say what such a project will require in general: the goal, precisely, is particular knowledge, local discoveries, specific attention. With this understanding, however, here are some suggestions:

1. Find a wild place within easy access.

By this I do not mean a national park or wilderness preserve. Wilderness proper—undisturbed land large enough to support wild animal ranges and ecosystems—is too scarce already, and can remain wilderness, of course, only on condition that almost everyone stays out of it.

But civilization does not steamroller across the landscape. In most places it leapfrogs; it leaves behind pockets of forest, wetland, small ranges of weeds and wildflowers. And development is not permanent. Land occupied by one generation is sometimes abandoned by the next, and begins the complicated process of finding itself again—finding the balance of circumstances and beings that will suit it.

In many places, then, there is the chance of finding a wild place, a place abandoned or overlooked by human uses: "the land is all small places," Gary Snyder writes, "all precise tiny realms replicating larger and smaller patterns." The first job, then, is to find one.

2. Commit time to watching the wild place.

The two provisions here, watching and committing time, go together. A stay of a minute or two will prompt the wrong kind of looking—the ignorant glance, the sizing-up and setting-aside. A stay of a minute or two might help, if you did it every day for years. But then the looking would have become study, and knowledge.

The other provision is to *watch* and not *do*. The exercise is to make yourself the lesser party, the one present by invitation, the one who must fit in. The stream or the wildflower is someone else's heirloom china; too much commotion will destroy it. It may be worthwhile to take along a flower book, insect book or bird book; even these, however, may be distractions, and it may be better to look hard and read later.

What are you looking for? Whatever is there.

3. Discipline yourself to look at landscapes in terms of human occupation and use.

Much specialist work exists to teach you to see the countryside this way. But you can start with this as simply as with a small wild place. The number, location, size and health of gardens is a place to start; or the layout, architecture, crops and agricultural rationale of local farms; or the difference in land use and land care between a suburban strip and a country road: you can begin almost anywhere.

4. Find out what bioregion you belong to and learn its ecological characteristics.

Bioregionalism is an idea long familiar among environmentalists. It suggests that we should determine our political and economic identities by the ecological systems we inhabit, and not the other way around. To a bioregionalist Michigan is considerably less important as an identifiable place than is the Lake Michigan dune system or the Grand River watershed. To learn a bioregion is to learn the topography, hydrography, climate, soil, plants and animals that distinguish it from the neighboring region. It might also be to learn the environmental history of the region and the human history of its landscapes. It means learning the large conditions of the small wild place you are watching.

Bioregionalism is sometimes linked, in the work of Deep Ecologists such as George Sessions and Bill DeVall, with religious options that Christians will find unacceptable—with worship of Gaea the earth goddess or of the planet itself. Loren Wilkinson is right to remind us of how environmental causes mix with heterodox mysticisms, of our obligation to keep our worship clear. If we do, however, then the surgery necessary to separate bioregional knowledge from pantheism ought not to be too difficult to perform.

5. Do some kind of subsistence work with property you own or have access to.

The range of healthy possibilities here stretches from radishes in an apartment windowbox to a garden 40' by 40', large enough to produce a year's vegetables for a family of four. Several million family gardens would have a palpable effect on the food industry. But we do not have to wait to have that kind of impact to begin.

A bed of geraniums, however lovely, will not help us here. It is not nature as ornament that we need, but nature as necessity, as the irreplaceable provision. For this even a small garden will do; and many of us, between the apartment and the farm, have room for a small garden. The millions of suburban backyards are enough; I watch for suburban gardens wherever I drive, and always see them with pleasure. But I don't often see them.

6. Do some kind of subsistence work in cooperation with your neighbors.

In a region of gardens, the local farmer's market and seed store become, as Dana Jackson says, hubs of discussion, advice, information and encouragement. Most of us do not live in such regions, however, and the times are unpropitious. (A slip in stock prices, however, as Jackson notes, is always matched by a rise in the number of Americans growing food; maybe there is hope.) We will have to look for friends, allies, coconspirators.

Country gardening is not the only possibility. The management of a woodlot may produce fuel to be distributed or shared, especially in rural places. There may be city possibilities, such as neighborhood composting of leaves or the location of small working gardens in city parks.

7. Make contact with the ecological saints in your region.

In chapter eight I called this neighboring an intact community. It would be nonsense, I think, for a Christian to learn the ecology of a bioregion and ignore the people whose livelihood and experience make them most at home in it. The nature of these communities, where they survive, will vary, and our opportunities to neighbor them will vary. You may be able to renew contact with a community to which you once were native. In other cases you may find yourself "joining" from outside, participating in part, looking on, listening. We have spent a century destroying these communities; we will not reconstruct them in a summer or an afternoon.

8. Identify the ecological sinners in your region and keep account of the harm that they are doing.

Christians are often reluctant to identify such people, under the mistaken impression that "judging not" means acquiescing to anything; and we are encouraged in this by the secular fashion for not "being judgmental." But we do not usurp God's right of final judgment or transgress against charity by recognizing the responsibility of people for what they do; and we abdicate our moral responsibility if we refuse to identify wrong actions or to dissent from them in a public way.

It would be a rare place, now, that did not have an environmental watch-group in operation. This suggestion may amount, in practice, to availing yourself of the accessible information and studying appropriate ways to respond.

The Minister of Gardens

Two chapters ago I argued that the environmentalism of American churches will remain slack and abstract until church members begin to take some practical responsibility for their own needs; and that local congregations—relatively small, relatively coherent, under the instruction (it is to be hoped) of a stable ministry of the gospel—might be the units of practical environmentalism as well as of theological.

I repeat these thoughts here because they seem to me to contain the best hope of a penitent and redemptive environmentalism in American Christianity. Biblical and theological thinking about these issues has received a good deal of attention, and both practical and educational agencies are at work in the church as a whole. It may be time to broach possibilities for individual fellowships.

A church might make itself responsible for a specific wild place (as churches in Michigan accept responsibility for keeping stretches of highway clean). It might include or insert produce gardens into its landscaping, food to be distributed in a food pantry. It might buy and work, or bring to work, an abandoned farm. It might commit itself, as a fellowship, to raising a certain percentage of its own subsistence, the supermarket price of the food to be donated as part of the church's giving. It might run its daycare and preschool in connection with its farm, so that part of the children's education might be a restoration of the natural sense we have lost. It might set out to train members as deacons of gardening or woodlot management or food provision on the basis of local production.

A number of agencies exist, now, to give Christians (and others) the chance to work, briefly, in Third World settings. An individual congregation might use part of its missionary budget to send itself, the whole fellowship, couple by couple or group by group, through one of these programs. (At Warner Southern College in Florida missionaries-to-be and others live in a Third World village to learn the arts of subsistence.) Healthy as such experience can be, however, we need to start with local concern and local attention. The first garden that the church grows ought to be in the churchyard. The first knowledge that it needs to discover and secure is what it knows about its own life. (The late Doris Longacre's *Living More with Less* [1980] is a model for practical wisdom gathered within a church community.)

A good deal of such work is already being done. It hardly requires saying, however, that on the whole the record of American churches has been abysmal. It is true with environmental issues as with others, that we earn (or fail to earn) a hearing for the gospel through our actions; and as the environmental crisis becomes more and more the possession of humanity as a whole it will become more and more crucial to our general witness.

Epilogue

A HOUSE BURNING in EDEN

Neither we nor any human, since our great first parents, has seen Eden; and the ones who saw it lost it soon.

Yet it is not quite right, either, to dismiss Eden as irrelevant. It is gone but its basic terms remain. Otherwise the stories of creation and of the tree of knowledge would make no sense to us. Every loved and beautiful landscape has some of Eden in it. Every culture more or less at peace with nature reminds us that we lived in Eden. It is in hiding all around us.

As with Eden, so with present nature: we are tempted by two contradictory attitudes toward it, both wrong. The rate of our exploitation and destruction makes us prone to sentimentalize nature. But we are also tempted to demonize it. Scientists and industrialists in the nineteenth century (and since) thought that nature contained the same Darwinian cruelty as the marketplace. As Liberty Hyde Bailey observed, however, the fittest to survive, in Darwin's scheme, is not the most violent. The fittest is the most fruitful, adaptable and peaceable. The saber-toothed tiger died out; the grass is still here. But will it be here when Exxon dies? For the houses we have built in Eden are surely burning; Exxon is helping us to burn them. By "houses" I do not mean culture only; I mean the niche in nature that we have been given to occupy, that we have partly made. Eden, inevitably, is burning along with us.

Turning Around in Place

The great difficulty and danger of the environmental crisis are that it is all around us. The technological culture is not one side or department of our life, whose excesses or mistakes we can fix with a law. It is our whole way of life regarded from the standpoint of how we provide for our material needs. Which is to say, our whole way of life: we think, write, teach and pray in the presence of the machine. Technology expedites thinking; and thinking is inclined, naturally, to rationalize technology. When you try to think about the system you feel caught in a circle: to change our practice we need to change our values; but to do that we must change our practice. We seem to be locked in a plane going down, with no alternative except to jump and go down faster.

My guess is that this is the dilemma of all cultures and therefore of human life itself. We are always at the mercy of our best ideas; and by the time we see their disadvantages these ideas are too powerful to be replaced. Even if this has always been true, however, our own predicament is new. For one thing, our best ideas have never changed the conditions of planetary life, until now; for another, the dominance of given ideas has never, until now, been so near to total.

The global village—when we do not really mean the global marketplace—means the dominance of certain ideas: beneath the differences of culture and religion (set aside as curiosities), there are the common principles—global capitalism, global technology, mass information. It has never been so hard to imagine an alternative, or to find a corner from which to state it.

The faith of the Scriptures seems, in our predicament, almost the only thing to offer practical hope. This is true despite the abysmal record of the church on environmental affairs. The gospel offers practical advantages because it remains always beyond our failures, and also beyond the reach of our best ideas. "The practical use of religion," Wendell Berry has written, "is to keep the accounting"—the evaluation of cultural programs—"in as large a context as possible—to see, in fact, that the account is never 'closed.' Religion forces the accountant to reckon with mystery."

But we can extend the uses of the gospel beyond that. This is the faith that clears the way for fresh ideas. It does this by requiring repentance and assuring us that the repented sin can be set behind us. Hannah Arendt saw the advantage of this in political terms: "Without being forgiven, released from the consequences of what we have done, our capacity to act would, as it were, be confined to a single deed from which we could never recover."

This is seeing forgiveness, however, as Arendt admits, in a "strictly secular light"; and a more fully Christian understanding would add two qualifying principles. The first is that forgiveness, being granted and modeled first by God, is always attendant on repentance—that is, it cannot be taken for granted, demanded or required simply as a human necessity. We owe it first to God to admit our errors and turn against them. But this is how we not only are released from our errors, but make room in our lives for the fresh idea.

The second principle is that neither repentance nor forgiveness necessarily or automatically releases us from consequences. We may repent and receive forgiveness and get started on a new track, and still have to cope with the consequences of our sins. Some we may be able to change for the good; this is, in part, what it means to make restitution. Some consequences we will not be able to avoid or change, and these we must simply endure.

What are the consequences we may have to face? The exhaustion of usable resources, such as fertility; mass famine and epidemic disease;

climatic change; the degeneration of our present technological infrastructure, as things wear out in the absence of energy and money to replace them; the poisoning of air and water beyond our capacity to tolerate it; the withering of financial resources based on cheap energy, as the energy ceases to be cheap and then to be available; the peril of political stability based on such structures.

There is no doubt, in any case, that our way of life will change. The question is whether it will change in an avalanche of evil consequences, or before it, because we have changed our minds: whether necessity will change us, that is, or whether, by repenting, we retain some freedom to choose a better way.

Vote Here

A couple of election days ago I drove past the fine, vital Roman Catholic church in the next town, and there were two signs out in front. One was the church marquee; the other was a cardboard sign on a short wooden stick, indicating with an arrow that the parish house was being used as a polling place. The marquee read: "Our citizenship is in heaven." The cardboard sign read: "Vote here."

The two signs and their apparent paradox seemed to me to get things just about right. *Here* is the only place where citizens of heaven can vote. Your heavenly citizenship is only as good, practically, as your earthly franchise. On the other hand, you will probably vote wrongly—irresponsibly, selfishly—unless you keep your heavenly responsibilities in mind.

But the two signs had another lesson. This is the lesson of size. We need, perhaps more urgently than anything else, a restoration of proper scale. We need to see ourselves realistically again, with our real powers, in our real limits. We have been assuming, for decades, that we are the giants of Giant Castle. The truth is that we are more like Aladdin; we rubbed the lamp and the genie came out. But he had the shape of a mushroom cloud.

Yet there is a difficulty with seeing ourselves in our proper scale: it has a kind of dismay in it. If we shrink our plans, will we not be too small to save ourselves and the planet in our care? If we try to relearn our true constraints, family by family and field by field, will we not be too late? The dangers are so large; the possibilities—if we discipline ourselves, if we refuse the temptation of big solutions—seem too small.

There is always a fallacy in hopelessness, however; and in this case the fallacy is a confusion of quantity with quality. The large solution is large in quantity: enough energy, money and know-how, enough unanimity among the voters, a big enough plan. The small solution is small only in quantity. It is large in quality: enough humility, enough realism, enough trust in the ways of created nature and in the One who made it. To entrust ourselves to these ways would be to do a small thing with implications as large as the natural energies of the planet, and the providence of God.

A Lily Among the Herbs

Regaining our proper scale means more, however, than repentance and obedience. It would mean rest as well. We could stop our everlasting goose-stepping in the face of the universe, and sit down to our dinners.

Someone recently asked me what I felt most strongly when I walked out into the woods.

"I feel," I said, "as if I were waking up—as if, maybe, I am sane after all."

"I feel," he said, "perfectly safe—as if nothing could hurt me."

Sanity and safety: that the characteristic feelings of the technological culture are disorientation and danger is evidence of how it has distorted the original outline of human life—of how far we have gotten from a way of life that we could responsibly claim to sustain, or even to imagine.

For this is what the human enterprise comes down to in the end: one person in the field, one in the shelter. One cares for the human link with nature, one tends the traditions of human culture. Neither work is possible without the other, neither is more important than the other. Both are carried on in response to our Creator, who made nature and formed the basic human institutions, and gave both nature and culture their fundamental orders. Both kinds of work can be done wrongly, in pride and greed; both can be done in penitence and gratitude.

Of course this is a symbolic picture. The person in the field represents all kinds of work necessary to a civilized society. Yet the image has a realistic force: if these kinds of work destroy the field—actual fields, forests, tundra, grasslands—then the enterprise is in danger. It will be clear, not only that the fieldwork is destructive, but that the shelterwork has been mistaken.

The reality of this danger dictates the scope of our response. We cannot repent vaguely or at large. Repentance is not an abstract or philosophical thing, though even philosophers (even writers of books) sometimes have to repent. It is a specific and actual thing: we must turn around in the place where we stand.

So: specific repentances, to begin with. Small, specific, concrete turnings.

In God's economy, however, small repentances bring large joys. A sane and secure way of life would be one in which our obligations would be underwritten by pleasures. The last place this was entirely possible was Eden, and the next will be the kingdom of heaven. In the meantime, though, the principle remains in force.

Small repentances; large joys. The old circuit riders used to say that heaven was a "Kentucky of a place." There are mornings, especially in late spring, when I think it might even be a Michigan of a place. Year in, year out, I go and stand among the oaks on the hill and just look and listen. When I come back to the house, I bring something we can use—a piece of dead wood to burn, a dish of black raspberries, a wild orange lily to plant among the herbs.

A
NOTE
on
SOURCES

As anyone who reads twenty pages will notice, this book has a group of what might be called tutelary spirits, writers who taught me to see the environmental crisis as a crisis of subsistence, and therefore not of "nature" in the abstract but of land in contact with culture. Wendell Berry, Wes and Dana Jackson, Donald Worster, Marty Strange and others belong to this group; and their work may be conveniently sampled in *Meeting the Expectations of the Land*, ed. Berry, Jackson and Bruce Colman (1984) (cited hereafter as *Expectations*).

Berry and Wes Jackson have been in my mind more consistently than I have had the courage to acknowledge in the text. But Berry's *The Unsettling of America* (1977), *The Gift of Good Land* (1981) and *Home Economics* (1987), among his many other books, and Jackson's *New Roots for Agriculture* (2d ed. 1985) and *Altars of Unhewn Stone* (1987) are basic reading.

Chapter 1: In the Aisles of Plenty
Dan Morgan's *Merchants of Grain* (1979) is a history of the international grain trade and its monopolists. Reay Tannahill's *Food in History* (1973) is a readable popular history; for more scholarly information, see the relevant chapters of Fernand Braudel's generous *Civilization and Capitalism, 15th Century to 18th Century* (Eng. tr., 1979-1984). For the general history of American agriculture I have relied on John Schlebecker, *Whereby We Thrive: A History of American Farming, 1607-1972* (1975); the story of American apple growing is told by Anne Mendelson in "Paradise Lost: The Decline of the Apple and the American Agrarian Ideal," in Robert Clark, ed., *Our Sustainable Table* (1990). As the American farm crisis has become more obvious, several good popular books have appeared, including Mark Kramer's *Three Farms* (1980, 1987) and Richard Rhodes's *Farm* (1989).

For the crisis in world agriculture and food provision, these sources have been helpful: Lester Brown, "The Illusion of Progress," *State of the World 1990* (1990); Brown, *U.S. and Soviet Agriculture* (Worldwatch Paper 51, 1982); William F. Browne and Don F. Hadwiger, eds., *World Food Policies* (1986), especially essays by Louis Picard and Nicholas Butler; David Goodman and Michael Redclift, eds., *The International Farm Crisis* (1989), especially essays by Frederick Buttel and Lawrence Tubiana; and the essays of Gene Logsdon, Donald Worster, Amory and Hunter Lovins and Marty Bender, and Wes Jackson in *Expectations*.

Gary Snyder is quoted from *The Real Work* (1980), p. 141; E. F. Schumacher from *Small Is Beautiful* (1975), p. 14; Gary Nabhan from *The Desert Smells like Rain* (1987), p. 106; Bruce Colman from *Expectations*, p. x; Donald Worster from *Expectations*, p. 33.

Chapter 2: The Marriage of Nature and Culture
Bruce Brown's *Mountain in the Clouds* (1982) tells the discouraging story of the Olympic Peninsula salmon. Michel Marriott described the "High-Tech Dorm" in the *New York Times*, April 12, 1991, p. A8. Christopher Manes's *Green Rage* (1990) is an angry and sympathetic account of wilderness activist movements. John Reader's *Man on Earth* (1988, 1990) is a very well-written and well-photographed sampling of human cultures, including always a consideration of subsistence.

Rockefeller is quoted from Alan Trachtenberg, *The Incorporation of America* (1982), p. 86; Leopold from *A Sand County Almanac* (1968), p. 101; Hardin from *Filters against Folly* (1985), p. 24; Neusner from *Ancient Israel After Catastrophe* (1983), pp. 51-52; Schumacher, from "The Age of Plenty: A Christian View," in *Economics, Ecology, Ethics,* ed. Herman Daly (1980), p. 137; Reader, from *Man on Earth*, p. 57; Harrington, from *The New American Poverty* (1984); Sewall, from John Wilmerding's *American Light* (1980), p. 292.

Chapter 3: Backdrop Thinking
J. B. Jackson's essays have been collected in several volumes, including *Landscapes* (1970), *The Necessity for Ruins* (1980) and *Discovering the Vernacular Landscape* (1984). He has had many followers, including D. W. Meinig, who is quoted here from *The Interpretation of Ordinary Landscapes* (1987), p. 183. Marx's discussion of "The Fetishism of Commodities," from vol. 1 of *Das Kapital,* may be found in *Essential Works of Socialism,* ed. Irving Howe (1976), pp. 133-44. John S. Taylor's *Commonsense Architecture* (1983), with drawings and calligraphy by the author, surveys "practical design principles" from many cultures. Ruth Cowan's *More Work for Mother* (1983)

put scholarly evidence behind the observation, made by many writers, that the convenience revolution did in fact make the homemaker's workload heavier. The way colonialism makes people into landscape was first called to my attention by George Orwell and the Caribbean-African revolutionary Frantz Fanon (*The Wretched of the Earth*, 1961, 1968), both, curiously, writing about North Africa. Harrington is quoted from *The New American Poverty*, p. 11; Hans Jenny is cited from *Expectations*, p. 48.

Chapter 4: Good Gifts

Edward Abbey is cited from his classic *Desert Solitaire* (1971), p. 266; Ananda Coomaraswamy from *Christian and Oriental Philosophy of Art* (1956), pp. 68, 70, 62; David Jones from *The Anathemata* (1955), p. 31. Dorothy L. Sayers's *The Mind of the Maker* (1941) is a well-known experiment in taking the creative process as an analogy for the Trinity.

Chapter 5: The Breaking of Nations

The Journals of Dorothy Wordsworth was edited by Mary Moorman (1971) and is quoted from pp. 16, 38. The standard account of Stalinist collectivization is Robert Conquest's *The Harvest of Sorrow* (1986). Marty Strange's *Family Farming* (1988) is not a popular history but a rigorous argument for a "new economic vision" of traditional farming (quoted from p. 33). Tönnies's classic study is *Community and Society* (Eng. tr. 1957); Christopher Lasch comments on Tönnies's ambiguous influence in *The True and Only Heaven* (1991), pp. 139-44. Witold Rybczynski analyzes the Ralph Lauren room in the opening chapter of *Home* (1986). Alasdair MacIntyre's very influential discussion of virtue and its traditions may be found in *After Virtue* (1981) and *Whose Justice? Which Rationality?* (1988). Brown is cited from *Mountain in the Clouds*, p. 234; Polanyi from *The Great Transformation* (1944), pp. 164, 224.

Chapter 6: Three Historical Examples

The basic statistics of enclosure may be found in W. Tate, *The Enclosure Movement* (1967) and J. D. Chambers and C. E. Mingay's account of *The Agricultural Revolution 1750-1880* (1966). The early stages are well retold in S. T. Bindoff's *Tudor England* (1969). J. L. and Barbara Hammond's *The Village Labourer, 1760-1832* (1911) saw enclosure as primarily an incident in the class war. Peter Laslett is cited from *The World We Have Lost* (1965), pp. 77-78; Christopher Hill, from *The World Turned Upside Down* (1975), p. 130 (Winstanley quoted by Hill in the same place). See also M. M. Postan, *The Medieval Economy and Society* (1972), chapter 4. The definitive study of rural violence in the early 1800s is E. J. Hobsbawm and George Rudé,

Captain Swing (1968). A brief selection from Friedrich Engels's *The Condition of the Working Class in England in 1844* may be found in *Essential Works of Socialism*, ed. Howe, pp. 58-63. Roderick Nash's *Wilderness and the American Mind* (2d ed. 1973) describes both ideas and environmental practice. John Stilgoe's *Common Landscape of America, 1580 to 1845* (1982) contains description and analysis of the early New England villages. Cotton and the Synod are quoted from Perry Miller, *Nature's Nation* (1967), pp. 35, 30. Alan Trachtenberg is quoted from *The Incorporation of America*, p. 53; Jane Jacobs defends the theory of urban centralism in *Cities and the Wealth of Nations* (1984). Wes Jackson discusses the Committee on Economic Development in *Altars of Unhewn Stone* (1987), pp. 99-102.

Lloyd Timberlake is quoted from *Africa in Crisis* (1986), p. 9. The two harsh judgments of the Green Revolution are by Angus Wright in *Expectations*, p. 150, and by Michael Roberts et al. in *World Food Policies*, ed. Browne and Hadwiger, p. 149. Andrew Pearse's study, measured but not encouraging, is *Seeds of Plenty, Seeds of Want* (1980). Robert Heilbroner is quoted from *The Great Ascent* (1963), p. 98, an early, optimistic account of "economic development in our time"; an early contrasting account is Sandra Wallman's *Take Out Hunger* (1969), which documents the difficulties of fitting an advanced society's notions of what ought to be done to a traditional society's workings. The comment to President Johnson may be found in Edward Wolf's *Beyond the Green Revolution* (Worldwatch Paper 73, 1986), p. 24. What has become of Mexico's part in the revolution is surveyed by Gustavo del Castillo and Rosario Barajas de Vega in Browne and Hadwiger, eds., pp. 153-68. Another study critical of the revolution but insistent on the capacity of peasant societies to change rationally is Peter D. Little, Michael M. Horowitz and A. Endre Nyerges, eds., *Lands at Risk in the Third World* (1987). Schumacher is quoted from *Small Is Beautiful* (1975), p. 192. Conor Cruise O'Brien is cited from Barrington Moore, *Reflections on the Causes of Human Misery and upon Certain Proposals to Eliminate Them* (1972), p. 114.

Chapter 7: The Cheap-Energy Gospel

My sense of the two-sidedness of American religious history has been shaped by William McLoughlin's many studies, including (for instance) *Revivals, Awakenings and Reform* (1978). Gerald Brenan's *The Spanish Labyrinth* (2d ed. 1950) is the classic account of older Spanish society, including the *latifundia* system. Thomas Berry (no relation to Wendell) may be sampled in *The Dream of the Earth* (1988), and Matthew Fox in many books, such as *Creation Spirituality* (1991). Robert Bellah is cited from *Habits of the Heart*

(1985). Two studies that I have found useful concerning the electronic church are Razelle Frankl's *Televangelism* (1987) and Stewart Hoover's *Mass Media Religion* (1988). I heard about Sermonshop in Patrick Ercolano's story in *The Detroit News*, March 15, 1991, p. 3F. Donald Davie is cited from *A Gathered Church* (1978), p. 21; Wes Jackson from *New Roots for Agriculture* (1980, 1985), pp. 118-32.

Chapter 8: Several Million Prophets

G. E. Evans is quoted from *Ask the Fellows Who Cut the Hay* (2d ed. 1962), p. 15; L. H. Bailey, from *The Holy Earth* (1915), p. 77; Gary Snyder, from *The Practice of the Wild* (1990), p. 61. Studies of alternative communities among us and in our history include John Hostetler's *Hutterite Society* (1974) and *Amish Society* (4th ed. 1993), E. D. and Faith Andrews, *Work and Worship Among the Shakers* (1974), and Priscilla Brewer, *Shaker Communities, Shaker Lives* (1986). The local memoirs mentioned in the text include John Haines, *The Stars, The Snow, The Fire* (1990), Gretel Ehrlich, *The Solace of Open Spaces* (1985), Ronald Jager, *Eighty Acres* (1990), David Kline, *Great Possessions* (1990), Donald Hall, *String Too Short to Be Saved* (2d ed. 1979), and John Leax, *In Season and Out* (1985). *Walden* is cited from the Princeton edition, ed. J. Lyndon Shanley (1973). Donald Worster's comment on Thoreau appears in *Nature's Economy* (1977, 1985), pp. 81-83. Berry is quoted from *The Long-Legged House* (1969), p. 140, and *The Gift of Good Land* (1981), p. 280. The concept of households is laid out most clearly, perhaps, in *Standing by Words* (1983), chapter 2.

Chapter 9: The Shelter and the Field

Loren Wilkinson et al., *Earthkeeping* (1980, 2d ed. 1991), is one of the most important guides for Christian environmentalism. The ideas of Nancy and John Todd may be sampled in *Bioshelters, Ocean Arks, City Farming* (1984). Snyder is quoted from *The Practice of the Wild*, p. 27. The basic guide to bioregional thinking is Kirkpatrick Sale's *Dwellers in the Land* (1985). Bill deVall's *Simple in Means, Rich in Ends* (1988) will introduce the reader to Deep Ecology from a partisan's standpoint, and also to the movement's religious experiments. Loren Wilkinson's warning is contained in "New Age, New Consciousness and the New Creation," in *Tending the Garden*, ed. Wesley Granberg-Michaelson (1987), pp. 6-29. Dana Jackson is cited from *Expectations*, p. 111.

Epilogue: A House Burning in Eden

Berry is quoted from *Standing by Words* (1983), p. 49; Hannah Arendt from *The Human Condition* (1958), p. 237.